If stones could speak
would they direct you
here or there
forward or back
around again the way you came?

Would they know you—
what you needed to hear
how loud or soft a voice to use?

Could they speak in tongues of fire and calm?

Would they ask what matters
as you walk among their shelter
or find cushion for your dreams?

If stones could speak
would their words
invite, warm, celebrate, reveal?
Would they warm you with pent up heat,
cool you with swift streams?

What strength, texture,
color, grit have waited
all their lives to greet you now?

Amy Webb
February, 2017

Stones at the Crossing

Aiming True
on My Journey
from Scared to Sacred

love,
amy

Amy D. Webb, PhD

Comments:
dramywebb@gmailcom

ISBN: 978-1-941069-77-6

*Proceeds from the sale of this book
benefit cancer centers*

Published by Prose Press
Pawleys Island, South Carolina

prosencons@live.com

For my mother,
and all who still teach me
to notice the beautiful moments,
right here, right now.

Contents

Preface

I did not set out to write this book. I did not choose the circumstances; they chose me.

It started simply enough. When the news hit, a wise friend counseled me about protecting a space for healing. From experience, she well understood the delicate balance of keeping supporters informed along the way, and engaging only when the energy said yes. So after initial calls to family and close friends to confirm my diagnosis, my contact was written in the form of email, and distributed to a wide-ranging group.

This was protective, on many levels. As I was trying to move through the myriad challenges and release of each new day, it was a relief to not tell the story over and over. But I did want people who would want to know, to know from me. And I wanted the protective grace of their prayers, from around the globe. Self-serving? Perhaps. I believed in the power of prayer to fortify me, even if not to influence an outcome. And I didn't want to just cut off from clients, colleagues, and friends. I needed their words of calm wisdom and positive encouragement, and I knew I couldn't have conversation after conversation, for weeks on end.

My first email to a couple dozen confirmed: breast cancer. Unsolicited, emails rich with information, resources, and help were offered in return. More personal exchanges began. The act of writing was about the only thing that felt normal or routine in my days, and it offered a time to be still, to be with myself, however I was. It was the only way I knew to record what I secretly worried would be my last days.

I wrote about the specifics of this life transition — the extraordinary but ordinary people, procedures, insights, and conversations that made a difference to me. And, I journaled about all the living and learning I did in between. I wrote about what spoke to me. About my earnestness to research and make wise choices, and my awareness that all the research in the world didn't guarantee anything. About tears of terror and gratitude. And the mystical connection to a much larger sense of life than I had admitted myself to on any regular basis. I noted signs along the way.

Paying attention deeply, and writing honestly from that immersion, became a way of working through the darkness — whether physical, mental, or spiritual. I came to believe that the process would clear space for a shift. I found myself juggling big questions about life and death, about what matters, about the relationship of *scared* and *sacred*. I could sit with my own creative process, and listen, weaving and interpreting the moments.

Writing became work I could do when I was grieving what I could no longer do. It became a source of healing balm, unawares. In the months when I couldn't voice coherent sentences, I could write a sentence that made sense. Even if it took awhile. Writing seemed to actually exercise my foggy brain. And, it enabled me to claim what was real: I had to be present to fully witness and record. No denial; all present tense. Yet, my past was present too.

Carrying Forward

At the outset, I feared nothing had prepared me for this journey. Thankfully, I was wrong. It seemed at the time that I had been torn in an instant from my life as a high-intensity professional to a none-too-patient patient. I had a lot to learn.

But I had kept learning journals since I was a teen, an irregular practice, a lifeline. I knew from my early career's research on how executives learn to learn from experience that regular journaling had real value. Some of those in the study resisted that work. They found that the candor required — about making mistakes, about what was new and uncomfortable, could actually intensify the emotions that go along with going against the grain. Those who stayed with the writing process, however, plumbed the patterns and the opportunities, and learned the most about how to get out of their own way and move into the new.

As a psychologist and executive coach for many years, I learned alongside my clients in the United States, Canada, and abroad. For over a decade, as an example, I worked with a small team of colleagues to conduct programs for top leaders of large organizations in the midst of downsizing. The premise of the development work: to lead others through transition, one needed to be able to lead oneself. This meant not just a headlong jump into the promise of new beginnings, but through the grief and muck and experimenting that precede those new starts.

We asked participants to write stories of how their world was changing—around and inside themselves. They then faced each other around a circle, and one by one offered the highlights of their stories. The unimagined happened. In taking the risk to share honest fears and hopes, they learned they were not alone. Lost and afraid in new territory, and admitting this to themselves and each other, the leaders found the courage to take the next steps. Recognizing one's personal truth in others' stories laid the foundation to become a community that learned together how to navigate the stages of transition.

The leaders were invited to create images, or metaphors, for this crossing together. One of the groups in Canada fashioned out of clay a symbol of a way marker — an inuksuk (*in ook' shook*). Unknown to me as an American, I soon realized that metaphorically, its meaning transcended culture. In real life, in vast uncharted wildernesses like the Yukon, Northwest Territories, and Eastern Arctic, the people of the land erected huge stone sentinels to offer survival support to those who would travel the same way after them. They marked rich hunting areas or caches of preserved food; they signaled a place of safe waiting, or issued a warning. These cairn-like structures were strategically placed, the stones carefully selected for fit: their size, shape, location, and direction mattered. The stones had to sustain a balance to be able to stand the test of time and elements. And the people shared stories of their meaning, so all who traveled could "read" the stones along the way.

The image planted itself in my brain.

Little did I know then how I would need these lessons personally. I expected my body to undergo a difficult trek, but had no clue about what my mind and spirit were signed on for. And there was no leader's manual for this transition!

Throughout my cancer treatments, I adapted some of the tools I used with clients to find my way and find meaning in the ordeal. I well understood from my training and work experiences that images and metaphors can release power. They can shed light when days seem dark, or spur hope when purpose and promise seem lost. They can reshape identity. I opened to these.

At a time when so much seemed murky about my future—whether I could return to the full demands of my professional career, what purpose my suffering would serve, whether I would live, the idea of sharing stories as way-finding helped pull me through.

Sharing the Way

Over the months, the purpose of my writing broadened. What started as a routine to ground me while my world was swirling began to help clarify my thinking. I reassured myself as I reassured others. I felt invited to risk more, to let my supporters intimately view from the inside out an experience most (hopefully) would never know first-hand. Choosing to be honest and open invited deeper relationship, and what initially felt to me like risk shifted unexpectedly to mutual gift.

Emails and letters to "dear ones" became more frequent. I included events, surprises, insights, or struggles that were representative of my days, recorded in journal entries. My circle of support expanded as people wrote saying they forwarded my letters to others in their families, neighborhoods, offices, churches. People I didn't know asked to be included on the distribution list that grew to well over a hundred.

I was truly humbled. What I documented as a glimpse into my cocoon had become something more for readers. The words that I sent out into the ether resonated with their hidden or not-so-hidden struggles. Some shared their own survivor stories. Some wrote to me about their own hardships and need for courage, hope, determination, joy. Some told me they were living more mindfully as a result, examining anew their choices and pace. Through their responses, I was blessed with the chance to see crosses and miracles in even more depth.

The journey through any life-altering hardship — whether cancer, trauma, a sudden loss — is not simple, but deep, intense, personal, unpredictable. The walk is not linear; it winds around itself, much like a labyrinth. There is a path before you; there is no getting lost. This is true even though at any point you may have no idea where you are, how far you are from where you started, where you are headed, or what holds the center. There is only the way in and out; the rest is ours to discover in the walking.

Ten years and major milestones have passed since my diagnosis. A passage far from clear and easy. Life in these years has brought key lessons into bold relief. Across those chapters of time I would review, distill, and cull over a thousand pages of writing to find a path through for readers. In *Stones at the Crossing* I share stories of what opened me and opened to me along my way. I invite you to read through the lens of what was true for me then, informed with a perspective of now.

But there is no prescription here. If you're looking for a how-to book or a resource directory, this book is not that.

Instead, *Stones at the Crossing* is an offering of my journal entries, letters, email exchanges, and essays, written chronologically, across two years. You will read of my experiences in walking the inner and outer landscapes, with the aid of the various healing modes and processes I was fortunate to access.

Although I believe that while each journey is different, there are markers and guides to help. My hope is that my story can speak to yours. Whatever life transition is difficult to navigate, when fear and grief threaten to blind you to hope, or asking 'why' comes up blank, this book may inspire new looking. When you wonder if you can find the capacity to not just endure the dark but also design a way through that honors your life, my hope is that these pages will invite and fortify you. If you are willing to walk into unknown territory, and learn to trust the signs of wisdom within and around you, you may find yourself equipped to meet what you never thought possible. God knows, we do not walk alone.

One
Opening Moments

Pasta and veal for Thanksgiving? Certainly not usual for me. But in Sicily, the meal tasted heavenly as we toasted to abundance that day.

The voyage to celebrate Pops' 80th birthday began a couple weeks earlier, flying to Rome and driving our way south. His parents were born in Sicily, and the pilgrimage to visit their birth towns was new for my husband, Richard, and me. For Pops it was a return to family roots, and to taste again some special stops he had shared with my mother just a few years ago before she died. The city of Agrigento was one of her favorites, he told us, sitting among the parade of ruins awash in autumn sun. I could feel her there, and I knew why she loved it. For a few hours, I walked paths so old that I started to imagine my feet in Greek sandals. And I realized I was imprinting the earth too, in my own way, by taking up the walk.

Our last week took us outside Catania, a citrus farm where visitors lucky enough to find the place can rent outbuilding rooms. It felt like home. Only better. Simple, natural, unhurried, unlocked. The cloth on the kitchen table was clean but faded, much like one in my grandmother's kitchen decades ago. In the center of the table, a large wooden bowl held some of the early crop of oranges freshly picked for us, along with a couple apples and one pomegranate, locally grown. *This is going to be just fine*, I knew, as I drew up my list for the grocery, next hill town over, at the foot of Etna.

One afternoon, the only one not napping, I sat myself in that kitchen, and picked up the pomegranate and a small paring knife. I recalled from my childhood how painstaking a process it is to get through the tough outer skin to the bitter inner membranes protecting the rich red insides. It was always worth the wait. I also recalled that as good-for-you as it was, this fruit burst forth and stained whatever it touched. That called for readying — an apron, newspaper to spread, and plenty of patience.

I opened out the top half of the door at the end of the table. My view through that window, a straight screenless shot to thick rows of orange trees, just out of reach. Every now and then a whiff of blossom made its way to my nostrils. Squinting hard, I could see the volcano's white summit yielding plumes of light smoke. It was a picture. Still life. And I was honored to be present in its midst.

Carefully I peeled in silence, with no hurried edge, no racing thought, no to-do list clamoring for a checkmark. While on the plane, I had read a story about someone asking the Dalai Lama to name his favorite of the many numinous moments he experienced. "Ah, this moment," he was reported to have answered. I got it now. At this table, with this pomegranate in hand. I vowed then and there to give myself more of these moments and to notice them with the relaxed awareness and focused ease I knew right here. Chunk by chunk, bit by bit, the arils were freed into my bowl, and my hand color testified to the labor. Time seemed to extend itself, protecting this space from interruption. When finished, I paused to savor. The mound of fruit would be shared, covering removed, freed.

When it came time for dessert that night, what would seem like an ordinary seasonal treat tasted unusually sweet to me. An extraordinary afternoon communion.

Pomegranate Moment Redux

Six weeks after returning home from Sicily, I felt the lump in my left breast. I was talking on the phone with my cousin, right hand tucked under my left armpit. My right palm moved just so and rolled atop a mass. Surely I pulled a muscle when exercising. Surely I would have felt something when I last examined myself. Surely distracted, I tried to focus on the conversation at hand — an update on her mother's cancer prognosis, her mother who shared my birthday and who had been like a second mother to me.

It took two days and a cancellation to get in for a late Friday afternoon mammogram and ultrasound. "I'll back you up with an appointment with a surgeon on Monday, just in case you need a biopsy," my gynecologist offered. Heart pumping hard, I drove home, and entered the endurance test of waiting. For the most part, the C-word stayed back of mind. I felt perfectly healthy. I exercised, ate well, slept. I had complained to my husband of being more tired than usual the past few months, but we both chalked it up to weekly travel, intense engagements with clients, working extra hard to clear the plate for the Sicily trip, the toll of jet lag, holiday rush. Just the weekend before I had cheered my niece who was performing in New York and walked her legs off on her first visit to the city. Tired was well-deserved.

Monday afternoon came way too slowly and way too fast. Richard stayed in the waiting room when I was called. Shortly after the nurse took my vitals, the surgeon walked in carrying my ultrasound pictures. I could tell by the look on his face that this wasn't going to be good. He immediately asked if my husband were with me, and Richard was summoned. "I'm so sorry to put you through this," I whispered to him.

I can't tell you much about what the surgeon said before he prepared me for the punch biopsy. All I heard was 'probable cancer'; he would have a better sense after the procedure. I don't know how many painful punches later, I sat up and tried to breathe in whatever normal breath I could free. An MRI was scheduled; I got dressed. I had to ask the nurse to write down the instructions for how to care for the biopsied breast. All words had washed through the sieve my brain became.

That night was one of the longest of my life, everything surreal. Tears stuck deep inside, until like a volcano they erupted and flowed and flowed and flowed. After what seemed like hours of alternating between wanting to be held and wanting to be left alone, I emerged from my home office and walked into the kitchen. The most normal thing I could do was to prepare dinner. This was a life rhythm that was familiar, a treat at least on the weekends when I was home to cook. I picked up my favorite paring knife and the bag of fresh okra I bought at the farmer's market just two days before.

Everything seemed to happen in slow motion, all senses on full alert: the rhythmic movement of the knife in my hand; pausing to watch an egret patiently stalking outside the kitchen window. In the silence, I could hear each segment of okra lightly plop into the nest of seasoned cornmeal in my bowl. And then I stopped. Cutting the okra brought back the vivid image of peeling the pomegranate. *Ah, this moment,* I remembered. A simple mindful act then and now served as food for my soul. I found in that moment a new hope: I could focus on the moment I was in, and enjoy that, and that would be enough. It was the life I had, still with me in it. Later that night I honestly had the thought: *Whatever time I have left, I will pay full attention.*

I won't tell you the week was easy. The confirmation of breast cancer cannot do anything but change everything. But I will say that when invited in, memories of peaceful moments and words that once moved me created oases of calm.

Present with My Lens

The weekend after my cancer diagnosis, Richard and I walked through Brookgreen Gardens, a several-thousand-acre feast of sculpture and nature three miles north of where we live. We chose to visit this place of magnificent beauty to distract ourselves from the ever-present but unvoiced questions about how much time we had left together. That weekend the National Sculpture Society Award winners were exhibited in two indoor galleries. From here, the exhibit would travel to New York.

I opened one glass gallery door and stopped in my tracks. To my immediate right stood a bronze female nude, my height, with her right hand on her left breast, thumb exactly at the spot where my tumor was. I struggled to breathe as I took in the power of this piece and the enormity of the coincidence. We moved slowly from sculpture to sculpture.

The subjects called to me: "I Am." "Waiting." "Expectations." "Grief." "Journey." "One Moment in a Waking Life."

Such true and intimate revelations the sculptors created! The timing of this exhibit, as though it were here just for me, as though these were companions of sorts, astounded me. Surreal. Heart-wrenching. Perfect. Whatever fragments of denial I had been harboring about the path before me vanished; these pieces testified that what lay ahead would be no ordinary piece of work.

I didn't take any photographs that afternoon, but a few days later I returned to pay my respects with my lens. I studied the pieces from different angles, capturing shadow and light. In visits over the next several weeks,

I faced each sculpture, shared a language that did not need words. I showed up and noticed: a familiar tilt of torso, a new line in a forehead, the weight of hunched shoulders, a hint of knowing smile. My experience was mapped in these forms; my photographs bore witness. The exhibit closed the day before my surgery.

"I Am" Sculptor: Ted Flicker

I decided to use these photographs to start a journal without words. These images, and those to follow, would do the speaking, as they had done in the galleries.

~~~

The presence of the sculptures fortified me. The sculptors truly knew the territory. These figures in bronze and stone, too, held a story. Experience became memorialized in something tangible, lasting, shared, that claimed, in effect, "I was standing where you are, walking this same path, and here is my learning."

With my cancer diagnosis, I lost my bearings. I forgot what in me I could count on. I lost confidence in my body. I blamed myself for neglect. I feared for what else I would lose. There could be a lot of new work to do and I worried: *Am I up for this?*

Now, my turn to decide whether and how to navigate this passage. I would keep my eyes open across the landscape to find what other markers might give light to the way.

Two
It Starts Here, Now

Just after my diagnosis, the head of an ecumenical quilt ministry at my church surprised me with a visit. She held in her arms a small quilt the women had made, each square knotted in the middle, and with each knot, a collective prayer for healing. The makers signed the back; some wrote personal messages.

I felt honored, but declined the gift, "Thank you for thinking I would need this, but I am ok; save this for someone who really needs it." I honestly believed what I said. I expected to have my lump removed, and to soon recover and return to normal life. Somehow seeing myself as qualifying for a quilt signaled a seriousness I was not ready for.

I was persuaded to at least hold onto it through my surgery. I took the quilt from her, mainly to not disappoint or seem ungrateful for the effort. So for a few weeks my cats nestled with me on it. I meditated with it covering my lap. I slept under it.

After surgery, learning that the cancer spread to lymph nodes, I knew I was in for a larger ordeal. Grateful for that quilt, I wrapped it around me instead of my denial.

How close I came to turning down this visible presence of energy and prayer! How little I knew at the time all I would learn about receiving and getting out of my own way. For months after that, friends and family signed the back of it, as a means to preserve their witness of my being lost, and found.

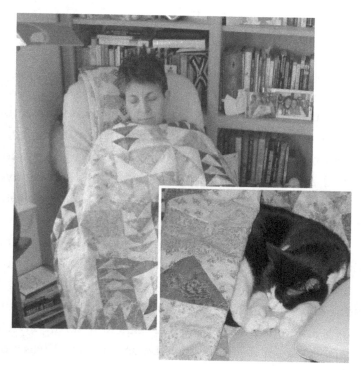

Such a Ride!

I hated roller coasters. Never liked the swirl and speed. I was always glad to have the ride end, to stand on my feet again. In the old days an E-ticket guaranteed the most complex ride, the longest wait. Not long after I reached the required height, I ceased wanting to spend so many of my limited number of tickets on so much upset. Sometimes you get a choice about what experiences to engage.

As a young child, I loved the family outings to Kiddieland, a dozen or so rides the variety of a full day's play. Only the roller coaster required my dad to sit with me. An old rickety wooden thing, about five feet off the ground, but plenty scary. He buckled me in and told me not to let go of the bar. We would start off level, then creep up, up, ever so slowly toward the crest. I always worried about sliding backwards on the rails, wondering how such little cars could be strong enough to carry us all. Once over the crest, it felt as though all gave way, a free-fall straight down and around, sideways tilts. I'd worry about no brakes, passing out, flying off. I rarely screamed, fearing that might make my terror more real. Besides, the air got sucked out of me without my effort. I remembered to breathe again when the rush was over. Walking down the exit ramp, that tower of blue cotton candy I begged for minutes before the ride held absolutely no appeal. I had just about enough energy to shake my head 'no' and sit for a spell.

I tried several times to ride much larger monsters as I came of age — more to avoid the ridicule from peers than any real desire—but as an adult I chose to sit and observe the multitudes dash to claim the first or last car. The thrill screamed out of them, hands waving in the air, as if paying homage to the tumble of upside down, inside out, again and again.

I chalked up my disinterest more to a matter of gut than guts. I just didn't like the feel. I wanted my stomach intact and my back without kinks. I lived fully and happily without missing that piece of action. Nephews, nieces, grandsons begged me to join while they rode "The Beast" and other terrifying rides. I held fast, preferring erect, poised, queasy-less. In hindsight, I never got the hang of letting go of that bar, preferring to believe safety meant holding on tight. But tight was never fun, and so neither was the ride. Just exhausting.

Two weeks after my breast cancer diagnosis, I emailed my nephew who was crazy about roller coasters. I wanted an image of one for my journal, thinking it just might be a fitting metaphor. I trusted his experience riding the most impossible of these, and asked him to choose one that spoke to him.

Instead, my nephew designed one for me, using some kind of incredible software he got for Christmas. This one had plenty of complex twists leading to two parallel loop-de-loops, and geography-appropriate palm trees lining the perimeter. Well then! I pasted it in my journal and thought about the ride to come, hoping against hope that it might be easier than the model that lay before me on the page. As days went by, I worked with that image, tracing the loops with my finger. I started writing about the ups and downs of anticipating surgery and treatments. Having an imaginary picture of a very real circumstance gave me an outlet, as well as a kind of permission to fill in the blanks with words too scary to admit to myself any other way.

I wrote about the climb. As my cancer treatments progressed, I wrote about the questions that put me in free fall. I wrote about the fears and guilt and anger and need for self-forgiveness that waited for me at the bottom and surprised me around the bends. This time, there was no bar to hold that would guarantee a safe ride. All that fear that had pinned me to my seat years ago came back in a rush, again and again. All I could do was be with it, surviving the best ways I could. God only knew how long this ride would be; I knew I was not alone in the seat. I started to learn with all of me how to surrender to the swirl.

Richard and I drove two hours to meet with a surgeon recommended for a second opinion. We agreed to keep our minds open. The doctor walked into the examining room, commented on my favorite earrings, put me at ease, made me laugh. He paused once, mid-explanation, when I sighed too deeply for his taste, at his descriptions of possible procedures. Waiting for the MRI to be copied, he assured and calmed me. He answered questions clearly, openly, offering counsel on questions I didn't even think to ask. His combination of heart and mind, so welcomed. As Richard and I returned to the car, I felt the first peace in a long while, and I knew I would be in good hands with him as my surgeon.

It took just two calls from loved ones for my internal doubts to start: *Do I really want a surgeon that distance away? Do I know enough to choose well? How many nodes would he take if the cancer had spread?* In a matter of hours I went from peaceful and resolved to upended, agitated and confused. Roller coaster indeed! That night in my warm bath, I prayed for clarity.

Next morning, a call to a friend who survived cancer decades ago provided insight and ease. I shared the questions flying about in my head, and in the process heard myself, my quest for certainty. As if a doctor would say the one thing that would cause me to totally trust, as if I asked enough of the right questions I could guarantee no doubts. I sat at my desk, mulling the questions, feeling the angst. It was then I saw the tiny Magic 8-ball next to my computer. When I turned it over, "Can't tell" popped up. I laughed and laughed.

Connecting Helps Me Land

A dream startled me awake at 4 a.m. In it, a longtime friend and I were sitting side by side on some kind of an airplane with its sides open. We were flying upward in a perfect Carolina blue sky. Seeing a jet passing in the distance, I wondered if we would hit it. She calmed me, saying, "No, it's too far above us." I looked down at the contrails and clouds below us, leaning out, and then fell out of the plane along with my seat cushion. I scrambled in the air to grab the cushion but couldn't reach it. I realized we were not as high as I had thought: *I hope I have time to get into the best position to land.* The cushion flew down and landed on a barn roof; I watched myself figuring out how to position myself to land. Then I woke up.

14

I emailed my friend about the dream, curious about her interpretation. Her response, vintage. She described her own total free fall into nothingness when she lost her firstborn daughter to cancer at 11 months old:

All kinds of fears and issues are rushing at you, and you don't know how it's all going to end. You never feel like you have enough information to understand and make sense of all the decisions you need to make. As time goes on, you learn more, and get a touch of control — over emotions, if nothing else. Cancer is quite a ride. You will ride it out with style and grace and love and a lot of growth.

Her words: the cushion for my landing.

A friend connected me with a woman from her book club who completed her treatment process three years ago for a similar type and level of cancer as mine. Initially reluctant — *Can anyone **really** walk in my shoes?* — I learned she was a retired nurse, whose volunteer schedule would make some executive workweeks pale. She was instrumental in starting a local breast cancer support group and offered to be my companion through my procedures. At least I figured we had a similar energy and values, so I agreed to meet her at a coffee shop.

I was still at the starting gate in all this, and had a lot to learn about the track. I had a page of questions and worries to discuss. Just as our tea was served, the front door opened, and in walked Richard, carrying two bouquets of flowers. Surprise! He gave one to me and hugged me. Then he gave the other to my "bosom buddy," saying, "This is three years belated, but I celebrate you. Thank you for being with us through all this."

And so a friendship was forged, life-giving for us all.

~~~

A colleague and friend offered to work with me by phone to create a personal vision statement for this wilderness period. She suggested this could be useful as an intention to support me through my surgery and beyond. I agreed. The process involved her guiding with questions and her noting verbatim my responses. She sent this back to me. I posted it on my wall, and in my heart. I read it daily.

At the end of this journey, I will feel satisfied if:

I meet each bit of news with calm fearlessness.

I trust my life, and my healthy body to support me as I heal.

I trust in the larger pattern unfolding in and for me.

I have made my needs and questions known.

I am accepting the path before me, and taking the next steps.

Listening with All of Me

My pre-teen niece sent an email today:

I want to be scared but I can't because I know you need me to be strong."

I replied:

I had an MRI today. I had to lie face down on a table, breasts in the holes provided, face resting on a soft pad with an opening so I could breathe. They rolled me into the middle of a huge machine that looked like something from outer space, making very loud and strange sounds. They gave me earplugs to wear. The imaging lasted for 40 minutes, so whenever the loud noises started, I played a game with myself, 'Name that sound.' One time it sounded like a jackhammer in the middle of a construction zone. One time, a washing machine. Other times, a dishwasher on the fritz. I heard rhythms in the beeping so I made up tunes—something you might have done with your talent for singing. In that tube, I had enough time to recollect our trip to New York City just a few weeks ago. I remembered riding in the carriage with you, watching you dance at Alice Tully Hall, lying across the bed playing cards. What fun we had! Thank you for these memories that helped me lie patiently through my procedure today. You are helpful just being you.

Keep writing to me. It will be good for both of us. You can feel scared and still be strong. I am scared, and I know I am strong. And we both have very strong faith. By the grace of God, we will have many more years of making memories.

~~~

His favorite motif these days (while I am living it), my nephew once again designed for me a roller coaster, this time as a Valentine's card. This coaster had the usual complexity of track but also a tall central loop, in the shape of a heart. I cried at the power of it. *Might this ride of mine be centered in heart?* I posted the card on my wall, stood in my room, raised my arms over my head, and bowed a gentle, *YES!*

I wrote in my journal: Holding on, no longer relevant. Opening to heart's wisdom, required. Each day opens to its own risk, but the biggest risk is to close off and collapse in worry onto the tracks, stopping the ride. I vow to fasten my seat belt and listen to my heart.

Finding What Speaks

Today I was reading through entries in a journal I've kept for the better part of a year. A couple months before my diagnosis, I had the privilege to lead with a team of dear colleagues an advanced leadership course for financial executives. Through various means, we invited them into a deeper understanding of how who they are relates to how they lead.

Early morning the last day of the program, I readied myself for my presentation on transition—the pattern of change from the inside out. I paused my mental rehearsal to take a few deep breaths on the patio outside the conference room. I noticed a yellow leaf larger than my hand fall slowly, gracefully, toward the ground, swirling up down and around, as if dancing. It stopped mid-fall. Crouching beside it, I wondered how it had moved as it did. How it halted. Maybe some law of physics operating. There was no apparent thread tethering it to the tree. With the leaf suspended but still, I waved my arm over it and felt the invisible line of webbing; it was reeled out from the high branch above. *Ah, that's it; I just couldn't see it.* I left the leaf as it was, and went inside to begin.

Without planning it, I ended my segment with the leaf story, demonstrating with my hand the journey of the leaf. I concluded by comparing the phases of transition to a three-step dance: separation, a middle way of neither here nor there, and emergence. As I continued I saw the attentive faces, the intense listening.

My colleagues later shared with me their verbatim notes of my words, and I wrote them in my journal during the plane ride home. As I picked up that same journal today, I found what I needed to remind me of the connection that carries me. Even now. Especially now.

As we make our way through, we need the curiosity to look closer, trusting the invisible thread that connects and guides us, enabling the dance. To understand that the phases are real and require different steps is part of the work. Trying to make the waltz a polka by hurrying the middle step doesn't cut it. The middle waits to be reckoned with. *It takes a fervent prayer for courage and patience to hang in there, while the faith that is needed to emerge is being restored.*

~~~

Messages I need to hear find their way to me. Sometimes I am paying attention. I overheard Richard's phone conversation with his friend: "Might as well live your life, turning it over to God, since none of us truly knows when it's our time to go, no matter what."

Later, an insightful email from a prayer group friend:

I think courage is acknowledging how scared you are, and plowing forth to take the next step anyway, as gracefully as you can manage. Emptying, and facing the fears and dangers of doing so, makes room to fill the soul with glory. Perhaps the monastics were onto something after all.

~~~

I called my nutritionist to inform her of my diagnosis. Initially referred to me by one of my clients, she has been working with me over the years to adapt healthy practices as my body changed with age.

We talked this time about how estrogen metabolizes in the body. She encouraged me to:
- Detox my system regularly.
- Supplement to fortify my immune system.

- Eat smart.

- Exercise.

- Reduce exposure to environmental toxins.

- Learn what factors in body chemistry play a role.

- Incorporate complementary health practices like acupuncture, yoga.

It sounded like a full time job! I listened. I committed to her that I would educate myself, make some changes, and take charge of my healing regimen as much as I am able.

I surrender to what is larger than me in all this. *Ah, such a dance between turning it over, and doing all I can.*

~~~

I am trying to educate myself as broadly and deeply about this disease as possible. A mound of books; hours on the internet. I have listened to survivors. But tonight I can't take in what I am reading. Fear drowns out the words; my blood pressure mounts; I start to sweat. I know I don't want to put my head in the sand. I know I have a responsibility to partner with the doctors and advocate for my own body. I know I don't have energy to reinvent the wheel. But I also know I have to honor what feels like too much. It's mine to figure out that fine line between informed and paralyzed.

I walk into the living room and choke out a request to Richard: "Can you read this for me and give me the highlights?" Not only does he agree to do it; he is actually eager. I have no clue how he struggled with feeling helpless in the face of all this, not sure what to do to be helpful. I trust his skill in research and synthesis. I know he will give me what I—and we—need, the right amount, at the right time. Courage is needed to bear the news and to ask. How fortunate I am to have Richard's mind and heart on this trek. I am grateful for resources I find and those appearing, unbidden.

~~~

My first restorative yoga class offered gentle body movement designed to enhance whatever healing process is underway. We warmed up with simple stretching, something that generally gets overlooked as my day races off. My body felt longer—something rare, being five-foot-two. The instructor spoke about how the body contracts in survival mode; the mind naturally drives a protective posture. But to move into a stance that opens out a courageous heart—my body found space to free its strength, inviting fear out of the driver's seat.

The next pose had us recline, propped on stuffed rectangular pillows aptly named bolsters, to enable our bodies to open and deeply relax. The instructor guided us in a visualization process. The invitation was to follow her words, take them in, listen. I was invited to imagine myself on a mountain, looking out. As I listened within, I received as a gift the word, *Oneness*. I became the image in my mind: the craggy peak at sunset with color on my face, the warmth melting my snow-covered crevices. As I looked down into the valley before me, I saw a composite of my women friends laughing around a campfire. They shared with me their laughter and their love. I imagined smiling at this image, and could physically feel my mouth move in a smile, real time, as I lay there.

"What is your heart's yearning?" the instructor finally asked. I listened inside myself for the longest time. *Calm Courage* came to mind. I knew at that moment I had found a mantra for my upcoming surgery and beyond.

In the final corpse pose, a practice of letting go, I heard these words from inside me: *I bring you tidings of great light. Trust me.* Tears rolled down the side of my cheeks and into my ears. I felt a peace I never thought possible facing what I never thought possible.

When I returned home, I took a 3x5 card out of my drawer, wrote CALM COURAGE in bold capital letters, and put it on my desk. And I wrote this in my journal. And I shared it with my prayer group. And I asked God to help me trust that what I would need is already there for me.

Yoga is helping me learn to pray with my body!

An early letter to my circle of support...

Dear ones:

I am leaving the state of numb, and bearing the weight of the steps before me. I have to remember to take it one step at a time, but walking takes HUGE faith. Not just accepting the reality of my cancer diagnosis, but the quicker-than-expected end to work schedules, income, and any sense of routine as I knew it. I am left to wonder, wonder, wonder about this new chapter ahead.

Today is the feast day of the Conversion of St. Paul, and the timing seems perfect. The first image that came to mind as I walked out with my diagnosis was the Caravaggio painting of this title I saw in Rome a few months ago. It loomed large on display, just recently restored. I was mesmerized, taken in by the power and humility of this surrender. Thanks to the internet, I printed out a color copy and taped it on my wall. I've been thrown from my horse. Surrender is what is asked of me now.

If it's possible to feel gratitude and relief, I feel that, since the initial news could have been worse. I am taking my place in the line of those who have walked this way before me, and are walking with me now.

I am just on the first step. I know you are with me, behind me. In the next days, I will need rest and quiet, so I won't promise to return calls right away. Blessed with so much love and support, I promised God I'd be a good steward of the time I have. I will make the changes I need to make to pay full attention, now that my attention has been stirred so clearly! Pray with me.

love, amy

Three
No Turning Back

On Ash Wednesday, Richard and I left the house at 6:10 a.m. to drive to Charleston for my lumpectomy. Unexpected heavy traffic even this early meant we would be a few minutes late, and I tried in vain not to stress. As we entered the hospital, I noticed its mission statement on the wall: "Healing all people with compassion, faith and excellence." As we walked down the corridor, I overheard another woman speaking to a nurse alongside, "I credit you with saving my life." A testimony most welcome as I start this process.

A doctor came in to apply topical anesthesia. She resembled my mother in looks, had a great sense of humor. I laughed out loud as she greeted me, "Oh, what a fun day for you—NOT!" We then talked a bit about things we can and cannot control. She offered this: "If you think you're in control, jump up and stay there." After laughing again, nodding at the clear truth of that image, I prayed I would remember this.

A friend had suggested I give up cancer for Lent. I thought of this as a chaplain came in to administer ashes and pray with me. This day a reminder that this earthly walk, no matter where it takes one, ends.

My surgeon entered the room, drew with his magic marker tattoos of circles and arrows on my breast to mark the tumor site. He voiced his concern that because of the tumor location, I may have a visible scar. We both laughed as I assured him that I can wear turtlenecks. It was clear to me that he needed to do whatever was right for the best outcome.

I don't remember being wheeled to surgery, but I do remember being wheeled to a hospital room. What was to have been outpatient surgery was not. With lymph nodes involved, the procedure was more extensive. I felt too numb to feel sadness or worry. This news, hard to absorb. My wish for no chemo, a short stint of radiation, was not to be.

Richard and his siblings were waiting for me in my room. He stayed with me all night as I moved in and out of pain, fitful sleep. Then, by the grace of God, I remembered my intention, and would center myself with gratitude: *Ah, this moment pain-free... Ah, this moment silence...Ah, this moment I can adjust my position to reduce the pain...* This vigil of moments became a prayer. When I got ahead of myself and moments of panic hit me, I recited my mantra, *calm courage*. I could visualize myself sleeping in the arms of God, and I could rest. Richard sleeping in the pullout chair next to me anchored me, too. I remember saying to him, "We are still here."

Equipped with instructions on how to drain the tube in my breast and how to exercise the side of me with fewer lymph nodes, we returned home. Next step was to heal and learn how to pull a treatment team together. I took photos. I walked. I tried to pay attention.

Soon after my surgery, my house filled with floral arrangements from near and far, each one unique, special to me. One morning sitting at breakfast I noticed the light on them and grabbed my camera. Periodically throughout the day, day after day, for as long as the flowers lasted, I took photos of their life. How radiant from within, standing in the light. How open. How exquisite the differences in petal and leaf as time elapsed.

I printed some of the photos, turning them into cards to thank the givers of bouquets using the actual picture of what each had sent. I would add a word or two under each picture, to let the viewer in on what moved me. On days when I couldn't do much else, or needed some quiet time, I would put on gentle music and sit at my desk and create. It didn't feel like work. For now, my energy, meager as it was most days, would be directed to noticing what presented itself, moment by moment.

All Forms of Messengers

I felt tired this afternoon and didn't push to exercise. Good that I was home to get a call from a friend. She reminded me she survived breast cancer against the odds some 20 years ago. It was so timely to hear her voice and get her wise counsel. She listened. She advised me to feel all my emotions, to express and work through them, and let them go. "Fear is the one not useful," she suggested. "Remember that your body is strong, that this is a blip on the radar." I so want to believe this. She doubled me over with belly laughter when she predicted, "Two years from now you will look back on all this and say: What the f--- was THAT about!?"

She proposed that by then I would know what had been opened up and birthed in me. She ended our conversation with an assignment: I am to say to myself, "I am healing," using all the love around me to help do this.

I will. I got off the phone and laughed again and again at her exclamation. I believe that question will be with me like a lifeline. Oh, to one day look back in amazement as I now look forward with uncertainty and hope.

Two weeks later...

I met with my surgeon yesterday to have him remove the drain tube from my lumpectomy. A tugging pain, short and sharp, but not bad at all. I was just glad to be relieved of it. He commented on how well I was healing and spoke some words about the likely chemo-radiation regimen the

28

medical oncologist might advise. Then he sent me on my way with a hug and my pathology report.

Deluding myself that since only two nodes were malignant I might escape the sentence of chemo treatment, I phoned a medical oncologist friend to read her my results. Her response, "No way no chemo!!" hit me like a ton of bricks. My heart pounded with the memory of losing my mother to cancer. *Would I, too, not survive my first chemo treatment? Would my heart and lungs, though younger, be able to take all this?*

Last night was sleepless. A rollercoaster of upset, fear, anger. It's an odds game, an odd game, this trading risk of big side effects for the possibility of a longer life. What finally calmed me early this morning was grace-given: the realization that I had no special deal as a human. *Who am I to think that I shouldn't suffer, or die?* None of us are spared; only the nature of suffering differs. I decided to deal with what's real in front of me. All of it.

I found trust not despair. I prayed, hard. I believed I would get the help I needed to get through. I accepted the grace.

~~~

Today Richard and I drove four hours to meet with a medical oncologist at Duke University to explore options for my regimen of chemotherapy drugs. She recommended a combo that may be less cardio-toxic than the usual protocol, given my fears, but the protracted period she spelled out for treatments made my knees weak. And she advised another MRI to clarify a shadow she saw on the scans. I had expected to soon be back working, traveling. I wonder if I will ever again have life as I knew it.

As we got in the car for the return home, I noticed a hawk on the telephone wire above us. I slept most of the way home. That much to take in is exhausting.

Tonight, my curiosity piqued, I opened a book on Native American wisdom and discovered that hawk represents the soul's expanding awareness. As symbol it suggests being swift and powerful in pursuing goals, being willing to view life from higher perspectives and see new possibilities.

I expect I will sleep better tonight, trusting that I will be given signs for how to walk this road.

Dear ones:

After my lumpectomy incision heals, it looks like I am in for six rounds of chemotherapy over the next 18 weeks, then a break, then daily radiation for six weeks. Hopefully there will be no lapse in treatment cycle due to low white blood counts or other unwanteds. The list of chemo's side effects makes me cringe. The thought of losing my hair on head, arms, everywhere, is less upsetting than other effects, if you can imagine. I will be staying out of the way of bug bites and germ-carrying crowds as much as possible during this period. I get a chance to practice every day my new mantra, "Calm Courage."

The good news is that I am healing from my surgery well, and am buoyed by all the love and support you send my way. I still can't resume normal exercise, and physical movement is limited, but I am making headway. Amazing how achievement now is being able to put on a shirt without help, or to stroll slowly halfway around the block. One step at a time, for sure, but I still can get into the kitchen to roast yellow peppers and garlic for dinner. YES!

Bless you all for caring so much.

love, amy

Two weeks after surgery, I kept an appointment with a patient at the free medical clinic where I volunteered. I wanted to make sure we had closure before I took a leave of absence as treatments began. Over the past year she had told me she lost her mother to breast cancer four years prior, prompting her panic attacks. I knew this conversation would be sensitive. So here we found ourselves sitting together at the precipice, sharing our fears and anxieties, the what-ifs. We reviewed the healing practices we discussed over time:

- breathing slowly and deeply;
- staying in the moment at hand;
- cultivating faith in God;
- reciting affirmations of courage and strength;
- informing oneself;
- experimenting with options.

A quote I read somewhere found its way to my voice, "God is behind you, but you have to do the work!" Each reminder to her spoke to me as well. We became mirrors for each other.

She read the poem she created for me as a parting gift. I wept. We sat holding hands and prayed. For healing, peace, strength. For one another. We hugged and promised each other to take the steps we needed to take, to accept the risk of being fully alive.

~~~

Today, another call with my nutritionist, to update her on the extent of planned treatments, and to invite her counsel on how best to fortify myself for the chemical onslaught. I took notes on her recommendations for what to eat, what to not. And we talked awhile about changes I might live with. She offered this gem:

"We each have in the wings of our lives these metabolic events, these points of fragility in our biochemistry. If we pick and sustain the wrong habits, these fragile points move from wings to center stage, eager for the limelight. Tell these elements, 'I will not entertain this drama!' Undertaking surgery, chemo, radiation is heroic, and then you are thrown into the rest of your life."

I sat in silence after our conversation. A long time. I remembered how deep water had always scared me until I learned to snorkel well, fascinated by the life below the surface. Time now to find the analogs to mask and fins and breathing tube.

Infusing Intention with Energy

It seemed right today to adapt my vision statement, to incorporate new learning. Not just a change of words, but with those changes, a shift of energy.

> *I meet each bit of news with calm courage.*
> *I trust my life, and my body to support me as I heal.*
> *I trust in the larger pattern unfolding for me.*
> *I have made my needs and questions known.*
> *I am accepting the path before me, next steps clear or not.*
> *I am a full partner in my healing, fortifying my body with nutrients and rest.*
> *My body is ready and knows what to do to reclaim sustainable good health.*
> *I feel positive. I choose life. I choose me.*
> *I am grateful.*

The friend who helped me with my initial vision statement offered to guide a series of active imagination exercises throughout my period of treatments. This process would help me explore how my own imagination could uncover images, or metaphors, to guide my steps. She would pose questions to invite my deep reflection. Today was my first visualization with her. As I sat comfortably in my home office, eyes closed, speakerphone on, she instructed me to deeply relax. We started with some long slow breaths.

She asked me what image came to mind when I considered my life now. I spent time with the question, breathing, until an image came into my mind's eye of a woman caught. Something looking like a mud dauber's nest absorbed her legs, but the top of her was outside the vortex, reaching for a branch with all the energy she had, to keep from being engulfed. I felt myself grow tired resisting the strength of the pull. My friend asked next what I could do, or explore, to change the situation. Again, I sat with the question. What came to me was a lesson from yoga class: I could adjust slightly, moving with my breath to create ease and space. I imagined myself bending, wriggling gently. My arm grabbed the branch, springing me from the hold. I was momentarily suspended in air, then landed flat on my stomach, arms strong and outstretched.

After a while, my friend invited me to project life at a point in the future. I named an imaginary date after treatments, and again breathed into the question of what image might depict my life at that time. The image of a black bull came through clearly, stunned me. I resisted the image at first, but stayed with it. With pointed horns, it used its massive strength to push through things that stood in its way. He was inside the bullring, ignoring the red-caped matadors backing away from him. All he wanted was to escape the ring that pressured him. I imagined him freeing himself, running unfettered into the street and eventually into a meadow. Again surprised by this unfolding image, I saw him standing in that grassy meadow with rolling hills in the distance, relaxed not raging, wondering why he was there. Several breaths later, I felt the peace the bull knew. He had used the strength inside himself to become free, content to wait on why.

My friend suggested I get a picture or some tangible object to symbolize my breaking free — the theme from both visualized images, and place it in my home as a reminder.

"The Wings of the Morning."
Sculptor: Marshall Maynard Fredericks

"Toro Bravo."
Sculptor: Charlotte Dunwiddie

The very next day, I went to Brookgreen Gardens with my camera. Walking through one of the outdoor galleries, I stopped in my tracks in front of a sculpture entitled "Whirlwind." It closely matched my visualized image of the woman in the vortex. As I stood taking a photo of it, I looked up and noticed directly across the courtyard a small statue of a black bull! I went over to "Toro Bravo" and snapped a photograph of this piece, too. And another of the large sculpture standing in the pond between them— the larger-than-life palm of God holding a human figure lying prone in it.

I printed the images for my photo journal, and in the journal with words, I wrote: I am amazed at how what I was seeking found me. How synchronous the moments if I open my eyes to see signs already here.

~~~

A week before my first chemo infusion, over a dinner of moving food around my plate, I confessed to Richard that despite my years of coaching leaders through their transitions, I had no clue how to do THIS transition. It all seems too big, too different a case. My memory of what in me is resilient has gone numb.

I washed dishes, something I could still do. Without prompting, my retired engineer husband with an intuition as vast as the sky, came out of his office carrying a blank white board, about 11x17, the kind that is erasable given the right markers.

He put the title at the top of the board: "Amy's Intentions" and dated it. Then he asked me questions: "What qualities will bring you through this? What qualities will you claim when you are through this? What will still remain of who you are?" He waited patiently for me to stop crying long enough to form answers. He scribed in navy blue my 22 words, capitalizing them, giving each space:

Vibrant. Strong. Determined. Courageous.
Robust. Present. Whole. Focused. Powerful.
Dynamic. Poised. Calm. Surrender(ed).
Engaged. Peaceful. Grateful. Joyful. Trusting.
Open. Teachable. Exploring.

Honestly, some were more hoped-for than something I was confident of being or becoming.

Then he asked me which were the few that I really wanted to focus on during this treatment time. I guessed: "Strong, robust, poised, trusting, surrendered." He put a dash next to these. His last question surprised me: "What one will be the hardest for you?" I reread the list, and quickly answered, "Surrendered." He nodded, knowing me. Next to this word he drew a smiling face, and circled the word.

Richard chose the spot in the kitchen to post this list where I would see the vision of it again and again. The process calmed me and turned the table on my fear. He picked up the pen when I could not. He remembered when I forgot. And for the next months my words and this process with him would inspire me, remind me, pull me, focus me.

Gathering Strength Together

Four nights following the Ides of March a few women friends gathered around my dining table to paint courage on their faces. I had emailed a circle of supporters inviting them to join virtually that evening and send pictures of the result. It was the night before my first chemotherapy treatment, and although I had done some serious mental work to be able to accept the option of injecting chemo into my body, I was still petrified. I can't remember how the idea of this preparatory ritual came to be, but a symbolic howling together into that dark night seemed appealing.

The six who gathered were diverse: two beloved sisters-in-law, friends from church, our former realtor. A few surprised themselves and their families by agreeing to do something so out of their comfort zone, and so public. Some others, who had hoped to join, canceled due to illness; ironically, a precondition for being present with me was being healthy. I didn't want my immune system to have to tackle anything more.

For weeks before this night, I wrestled with how to approach cancer treatment. Fight or surrender? Yes, both. A powerful executive client urged me: "This is not the time to surrender [meaning, to give up], but everything in you must fight; don't let us down." Perceptive as he is, he knew how to press to get my attention.

A wise friend who has survived cancer for 20-some years cautioned me against mustering negative energy, or using language that would signal a battle against my own body and what it needed to survive. The confusion and fear about all this nearly paralyzed me. Thanks to good friends and my priests, and plenty of prayer, I found a blend. I settled into a view that allowed me to move forward: committing full-out, fighting any urge to give up while accepting what is before me, acknowledging the limits of my control. Choosing to give up resisting. Finding the strength in vulnerability would guide the fight.

What might have been a war party became instead a kind of celebration of intention. All that I had within me, and within those attending near and far, would be directed toward affirming life, and calling forth my potency, to ally with my chemical agent. This gathering of fellow warriors stood together as one, imploring the agent to do its work efficiently, targeting true. The evening's invitation to take a risk, participate, paralleled the very vulnerability that we were symbolizing.

I set the stage. A few hours before the women arrived, I selected a few CDs of Native American music, wrapped the glass tabletop in flip chart paper, and set out pens, paints, mirrors, eyeliner. A dear friend joining virtually from Colorado had sent a supply of face paints the day before: "Count me in; I'm with you, sister," she wrote. Bowls of water and brushes were spaced around, and a few towels. In the middle of the table, I posed my warrior woman symbol given to me years ago by another close friend and colleague. She stood four inches tall, clad in colorful armor, with a shield in one hand, and a sword in the other. I laid her plastic crossbow at her feet. At 7:00 p.m., the doorbell rang.

I'm sure if I had polled the group, everyone would have admitted feeling tentative, maybe even foolish, but stouthearted nonetheless. Those who wanted to be relaxed by wine, poured forth. It humbled me to take this in — these, and many others virtually, gathering for ME, with me.

The only request I made to guide the activity was for each person to come up with a quality they would grant me to support my way through the treatments. We began. I read a prayer my aunt had sent. Slowly the process unfolded. Some immediately started painting. Another sat and planned a design, staring long in the mirror at her unpainted face. Two painted finishing touches on each others' faces. Hair got streaked. I mixed a unique bright red-orange, and painted my chin, remembering what it can mean to stand up to something tough. I took some photos through the process. We laughed amidst moments of concentrated silence. As we finished, the changes on the faces around me took my breath away. In an hour these women had transformed into warriors, fierce and powerful.

Dark outside, we lit candles around the table and turned off the lights. I asked each woman in turn to announce the quality or image she would have me take to treatment. I wrote each with a marker on the paper tablecloth. I half expected names like "Savage Princess" or "Dragon Slayer," but instead heard: "Happy Dancing Feet." "Comet Woman, Soaring across the Sky." "Courageous Fortified Spirit." "Friend of Love." "Sparkle Bird." "Poised Princess Ready to Grow."

Fitting names, given this feminine circle. Then in silence we allowed the names to echo in our minds and hearts. The soft chanting and drumming music in the background, a worthy accompaniment. Tears flowed. Without having to coax, we all stood and stretched arms wide to reach each other around the table. We threw our heads back and howled into the room, filling the house and beyond, once, twice, three times, together. Each time louder, more impassioned, with an inner intensity none of us would have imagined.

I'll never forget that evening. Richard returned home from visiting a friend in time to take some group pictures. Everyone embraced, then left with faces still painted, promising to drive safely, lest they'd have to explain their looks to a policeman. They wished me well, and thanked me for the experience, which surprised me. I hadn't expected this night would open each woman to her own voice in a new way. A collective release. As I cleaned up, I tore off the section of paper on which I had scribbled the qualities.

And I sat with it on my lap for the longest time, in the quiet, with only the candles for light.

The next morning I went to my treatment, rested and ready — or at least as ready as I could be. I had packed in my tote the recommended water to drink, rice crackers to eat, something to read, a photo of Mendocino where Richard and I were married, an array of stuffed animals sent by loved ones, and the scrap of table covering with names. I about fell out of my recliner as the oncology nurse wheeled over the toxic cocktail — it was exactly the red-orange that I painted on my chin the night before! Immediately I recalled my face in the mirror, and breathed in that powerful communal energy once more. *Dragon juice, go to work*, I instructed silently, eyes tightly shut.

As the liquid made its way into my port, I held the hand of my bosom buddy who sat with me. I told her about the warrior party, the one here at my home in Pawleys Island, and the ones I learned about in Racine and Greensboro and Denver and Boston and London and Haifa and New York.

Dear ones:

The reality of the upcoming chemotherapy, radiation, and drug regimen is daunting. I keep your support close. I visualize it as a flying carpet I can ride on through the next months, along with my strong faith, and belief that all things do work for the best. Much as I wouldn't have ordered this journey, I am finding myself grateful for the time to experience moments fully. Whether up or down, they are all mine to live, wrestle with, appreciate, transform.

The mystery that is life unfolding is calling me to take deep looks at the most important questions. Thank you for your continuing prayers, stories, and hope.

love, amy

Four
Wandering Into Deepest Dark

For a good while I couldn't bring myself to tell my 15-year-old niece that I had cancer. All those self-protective defenses get called up in the name of protecting someone else. When the post-diagnosis path was clearer, I told her that I would be getting chemotherapy and would likely lose my hair. All of it. After she gathered herself, we talked on and on, about what will change, and what already changed. I confided that I was planning to shave my head before the predicted clumps fell in earnest. Immediately she begged: "Can I come for spring break? Can you wait to get your head shaved until I get there?" And so it happened.

Losing hair is change made visible. And while not everyone loses hair from cancer drugs, many do—at least temporarily. Some survivors told me about how their hair grew back darker, lighter, curlier, straighter, a different color. Or in patches, or not at all. So I didn't know what I was in for, which called for a ritual.

For years I complained about a curse of bad hair, generally worn short. Stick-straight, two cowlicks, and a widow's peak challenged the best of stylists. I wasn't sure that losing it was all that bad a thing, provided that something better grew back. Rationalizing can be helpful in small doses. I went with my sisters-in-law to pick out a wig in case I wanted to wear it outside the house, thrilling my husband with the notion of living temporarily with a redhead. And then I waited.

My niece arrived two weeks to the day after my first chemo treatment, the first strands of finished hair having strayed on my pillow the morning before. As I showered, my hair started falling into my face, and I couldn't rinse it, rinse it, rinse it from my hands after shampooing. It was time.

I made a last call with hair to a dear friend. As we talked, she reminded me of a gift she had sent. I lifted the thin book from my shelf and opened it randomly, eyes landing on the story by a woman with cancer just having shaved her head. Amazing, this synchronicity! I read it aloud to us, pausing at the parts that made us both stop to catch our breath.

Driving with Richard and niece to the hair salon, I was aflutter. The usually long twenty-minute drive seemed way too short this time. In the chair, under the cape, I braced for the cold buzz. Attachment #4 — to get as close to the scalp as possible, careful to avoid any nicks. I closed my eyes and felt my past life fall down my eyelids and cheeks. Only the sound of shaver in the room, for minutes on end. When my stylist finished, he turned the chair so I could face the mirror. "Whoa," I grimaced. "I like it," my niece said. "You look strong. Really." I'll never forget those words. Richard took pictures of the moments. He came over and hugged me beautiful, and then sat in the chair. His turn. His choice that we would resemble twins.

When we returned home, my niece angled the camera to capture a silhouette of the two of us shorn. It became the first photo I emailed to the widening circle of people supporting me. Besides cooking, laughing, reading, bicycling, and talking with me this week — albeit at a reduced pace for both of us, my niece was able to accept the changes in me. She claimed no embarrassment to be seen with me dressed "like a mad scientist" as we walked under the sun.

She left the next afternoon, Holy Thursday on the Christian calendar. At church that evening, at that re-enactment of brokenness, humility, and invitation, I read the scripture for the first time hairless in front of my fellow parishioners. I chose to go wigless, but for warmth wore a hat sent by a colleague. A rather plain one, cream with roses, soft, my head so sensitive to the touch.

In the next weeks, without my prompting to do so, friends printed and posted that photo on computers and refrigerators and prayer altars, and then wrote to tell me. Initially through the eyes of others, I came to see myself new. Strong. And what got birthed in me was a willingness to risk exposure as never before. Not just a head that now gets colder quicker. Not just sharing that photo with clients with whom I recently wore serious suits and for whom I tried never to have a strand of hair out of place. But the risk I took was being open to being seen as sick, different, less-than. Or getting better.

Dear ones:

Today, a change. After waves of wrenching nausea day after day from my first chemotherapy treatment, I was able to eat a light breakfast, take a walk in glorious spring air. I have to be covered up totally, but my red floppy-brimmed Italian sunhat and black sunglasses outfit me just fine. The next few months I am choosing to live indoors a lot, selective about what I do and who can visit. Limiting the exposure to germs. That will be a challenge.

I want to go kayaking but have only enough energy to listen to CDs. Having the time to listen to music is a real treat, though. Who knows how the cycles will unfold? The doctors tell me what to expect, and that everyone's course is different. Amazing what my learning curve entails now.

love, amy

Abundance of Heart

I didn't set out to collect any covering for my hairless head. I figured the summer heat and my being mostly indoors didn't require headgear. Richard didn't mind the bald look, and once I got used to believing that it was still me in the mirror, I surrendered. In fact, I loved being freed of make-up and other face-saving ablutions I have done to be presentable, to appear more of myselfs Au naturel meant less risk of infection; but my head got cold at night, and my scalp flushed under the sun.

I only ordered two hats for myself, one flannel nightcap to ease the friction with my pillow, and one to wear to doctors' offices, which typically refrigerated me. But one of my dear friends had a wild hair one day, and without my knowing, invited my email list of angels to surprise me with hats. She apparently encouraged them to be creative in their selection, making a personal statement of sorts, customizing what they imagined would give me comfort, or a good laugh. I learned about this only when a few started arriving, out of the blue. She fessed up.

For weeks, all variations of head coverings rang the doorbell and got carried across the threshold. Floppy-brimmed sunhats — navy, or periwinkle with white polka dots. Canvas boat hats with flowers. Ball caps of different colors — hand-decorated, embroidered with HOPE, even one in sequined camouflage from a Harley riding client. Silk scarves. Repurposed t-shirts with rows of ladybugs or watermelon seeds, drawn with permanent markers. A crown of dried flowers to wear with a pink feather boa. Special knit ski caps for chilly morning walks.

And stories came with them. Like my brother being asked in a Paris airport security line what he had in the package. "Wish her well for us," he was told after showing them the latest style black straw fedora. Only my brother. A client's child picked out a souvenir cap for me on his spring break at Disney. A friend carried one back from Australia where her grandchildren routinely wear that sun-limiting kind to school. A client in Europe sent a light blue wig with curls down to my stomach, complete with a video of his well wishes while his office mate modeled the prize.

One day I opened a box with a leopard-print hat inside, and another wrapped in tissue paper. It was a shaggy smooth nightcap, with a note from the hat-maker: "We have gotten so many orders for you, we thought we'd join the chorus in sending you best wishes." I was floored.

I made choices each day about wearing one or not. Matching or not. The selection taking into account how much of my head needed to be covered or not. Maybe it was my imagination, but when I wore one, I felt all this love coming down through the top of my head to fill me, fill me, fill me. I guess that's what the senders had in mind; many wrote that this chance to participate tangibly in my healing meant much to them, too. Abundance shared. Humbling to know so many are throwing their hats in the ring with me.

Once a month for years I met with two women friends for tea, to catch up on our lives, and to help each other hear what we need to hear. Through my cancer treatments, this connection became more episodic. This morning the conversation took an interesting turn. My friend asked a rhetorical question: "Am I allowed to *expect* abundance?" I asked for silence, to absorb the question, its implications.

At one and the same moment, I felt challenged, relieved. *Do I honestly live from a place of expecting abundance, not scarcity? What in me holds back, withholds permission to live life as a miracle unfolding?* I remembered some version of the Einstein quote, "There are only two ways of living your life. One is to live as though nothing is a miracle; the other is to live as though everything is a miracle." I left that conversation feeling grateful, reflective. *How might my days be different, even through this, if I allowed myself to expect abundance?* I promised myself to experiment with the shift and see what opened.

~~~

Sadness and fear come in waves. Mostly I am upright and strong, but moments of wondering and worrying overtake me. Sitting with Richard today, my emotion tumbled out, "Tell me I am not going to die with this!" I pleaded. He held me. I cried and cried.

It feels like chaos. *Nothing seems the same as it was. Am I allowed to hope? What does abundance look like now?*

~~~

When I came home from early church service this morning, Richard was still asleep. I went into my office and wrote a poem, to thank him:

He sees beyond the gaunt dark-circled face And calls me beautiful.

He kisses my bald-fuzzed head And calls me his principessa.

He laughs at my illusions And offers me hope and truth.

He sits with me to hear next steps and news And paints my surrender.

He builds me a soft table And invites me to lie down for massage.

He listens beyond my complaining And hears the sounds of this passage.

He understands my awakening And holds his lantern next to mine.

Blessed in Exile

How do I get through this wilderness, this wasteland? All I know is I need to fight to stay in the game, whatever that entails. To stay focused on healing. To be true to myself. To honestly feel what I feel. Good, bad, ugly, up or down: accept it all. This is the work I am called to do right now.

And yet, I feel intensely the loss of what I knew: the work I can no longer do, at least for a while, and the absence of income, the prospects of starting life over.

For decades in private practice, I've paid premiums for temporary disability insurance, to cover emergencies that would prevent my working. I spoke today with the specialist from that insurance company. She wanted to know the chronology from day of diagnosis, the details of doctor visits, last days worked, and then some. The recalling was difficult—so much to retrieve, so much to relive. I found it really hard to explain to someone who had no clue about the opening salvos of a cancer journey: the volume of things to be done, the day-to-day ambiguity of waiting to hear about appointments, the preparations needing full attention, the moment by moment undoing-redoing-undoing of plans and schedules. Such a contrast to life just weeks ago when most work commitments were firmed up months in advance.

As the phone call continued, my frustration with her ignorance turned by the grace of God: *How COULD she know? How would I have ever known?* She needs to understand my situation fully to determine if financial support can be offered, even while I am trying to get my own arms around the situation. We both deserve compassion. I know my job right now is to take care of me, but I feel like I am in exile from the producing world. The waiting, the not-knowing where all this will lead, is overwhelming.

Grateful for a friend's words remind me of what I can do: "Keep breathin', baby!"

Early this evening, Richard was home with me as we opened our door to an unexpected visit from friends. One, a priest, came by to offer me a blessing. At first a bit self-conscious, I accepted.

I sat on a chair in my sunroom. He asked for candles to be lit while he vested, then read prayers aloud. He invited all hands onto my shoulders. I closed my eyes. Under the warmth, I cried at the sacred mix of power, vulnerability and gift in this act. We shared the Eucharist. Then an anointing with oil. I tried not to think of this as last rites. But so be it. Within a few minutes, my palms and forehead became hot to the touch. I felt calm, lighter, as if something inside had surfaced and released.

That heat lasted long after our guests departed. My hands, rarely warm now, folded around my prayer tonight, *As I am, I go forth. Thanks be to God.*

Forgiving Myself

A few days later, I worked on putting together the information I needed for my temporary disability claim. Richard helped with locating and printing invoices for the year prior to diagnosis. I wrote detailed descriptions of the nature of my practice, its pace and scope, days of travel, week by week, month by month.

By the time I got five months into my calendar, I was stunned at what was appearing in black and white before me. First quarters of a year were usually busy, but even in a year with a deliberately reduced load, I traveled most of the time. And, I volunteered as a counselor in the free medical clinic, and began to build local work options and contacts for the future to ease my travel. I took deep breaths listing all that activity. The stress and toll of that continuous pace sent signals I overrode for years. I saw how big a jolt might have been required to cause a shift in my normal. Just a few days ago I had to answer the surgeon's question about the date of my last mammogram. I thought it had been a year, two at most, but it was four, seemed like yesterday. I kept postponing, accommodating changes in client schedules and travel options. Now, facing all this evidence of hard driving, all this unfettered truth, I sat and sobbed. Forgiveness work awaited me.

~~~

While Richard cleaned and waxed outdoor sculptures at Brookgreen Gardens, I sat in a chair, all covered up from the sun. I simply didn't have the energy to help him with his conservation work today. Instead, I chose to write a poem in memory of my mother. I realized that in all our years here I never have taken an afternoon to just sit and write in these gardens.

Dear ones:

The rhythm of all this is a mystery that fully draws me. Each cycle is different, but I've found that in the first days after a treatment, my focus is on getting through, enduring, recasting a routine, giving in when the plans I made seem too much. My priority is to surrender to what my body needs; I am learning to tune in much better to what and when. I am not pressing myself to produce or think so hard—what feels right is to treat gently this self of mine that is trying to come back through the dark.

Then, starting a week or so in, I get the glimpse of "OK, we're coming back around now." Stomach intact, skin and scalp not as sensitive to the touch, vision less starred, breath less short. Despite days of not being able to will my eyes to open, there comes a time to shift. I am trying not to push, or launch aimlessly into activity when I get my first oomph of energy. And there is plenty of opportunity to forgive myself when I fail at this.

But I am also not sitting idly. This time seems like a rich period to focus on the questions: **What will I do with this day? Why am I called to be here now, in this space? What can I learn about being me here that will become a gift of this time?** I balance quiet and active, solitude and engagement. 'No' becomes easier now. I am admitting to finite energy, and am learning what drains and what fills me. It seems critical to my healing to be faithful to myself and honest with others, in what I say yes to, moment by moment.

It felt so good yesterday to be able to go outside and transplant flowers and seedlings. With gloved hands in the dirt, I could focus on growing things.

love, amy

Giving and Receiving as One

After this morning's healing service at a neighborhood church, a woman introduced herself to me. We continued to stand together and talk a good while in the parking lot. I was not a member of this church, but she welcomed me warmly. She told me how she moved here because she loved to play golf, but a few short months into her relocation, her severe arthritic condition worsened. She turned to rose gardening. We talked about best-laid plans, how so much mattered about how we dealt with Plan B. She offered to visit me; I gave her my address and phone number.

Not on any regular basis but for weeks, she visited, bearing the gift of her. She'd leave a note if I weren't home, or weren't feeling well enough for a chat. All I could offer in return was my joy and my sheer willingness to receive.

Amongst the cycles of poison and pain
what rises through the body
is the warmth
of your smile at my door
carrying in your gnarled fingers

a vase —
that plastic water bottle
simply changed,
still useful, to hold
me
in the bouquet of roses
the colors of sunrise
you grew in your garden
since you could no longer play
the music you planned to live.
Your turn at surrender,
now mine, find us—
yesterday's strangers
on my front porch
hugging our saving grace.

Over the years, I volunteered to speak at workshops given for people transitioning to retirement. A fellow colleague took my place and offered her time and expertise in the same workshops when I was sidelined with treatments. Today an email exchange with her.

All the things you've talked about so powerfully, and coached others to do so effectively, are the things you need in order to face your own transition now. Replay the videotape of your presentation. Don't doubt your own knowing. Dare to hope. You are wearing the ruby slippers! Click those heels and flap those wings, baby; it's time to haul ass back home!

I laughed out loud, and emailed back:

It feels like my whole life has been preparation for this time, tools and insights at the ready if I remember to look. You are right to remind me to tap in, to not doubt I already have what I need, or will be given it. I am smack in the middle of the wilderness now, with some aspects of my life still ending, and some beginning to begin. It requires all these parts. It's painful to hold onto the illusion that transition should be one unchangeable state of beginning. I promise to choose life without a doubt.

Dear ones:

I am receiving what I need to get me through. I am trusting this more and more. This cycle, good physical energy, minimal side effects, injections to boost my dropping red cells; foods like almond butter, coconut milk and avocados to stem the tide of weight loss. And perfect spring weather for early morning or evening walks. I continue with my cooking, experimenting with use of ingredients as obscure as teff flour, and as sublime as fresh beets and greens from a friend's garden. I believe these will likely be part of my new life regimen for years to come. With so many delicious and healthy things to eat, I hardly feel deprived. My eyesight cleared more this week so I could return to my photo journal.

With a coming change of chemo drugs, I probably have only a month of eyebrows and lashes left. I am wearing all my hats, and am getting quite used to looking in the mirror hatless and seeing ME, not a stranger. I've been given the grace to feel calm and loving toward that self. I wouldn't trade my life for anyone else's right now. To be this aware of the life-giving elements of each day, and how spiritual a journey this physical challenge is, I am fine. For whatever time is mine, I give thanks.

love, amy

Pain Meets Gratitude

I spent the last four days in bed with body aches, feeling wretched. I am tired of the dragon juice. A friend called today and suggested I pay homage to that chemo—"it was dirty work but someone had to do it, and Big Red the dragon stepped forward." It's hard to feel grateful for what makes me feel so bad, but I AM grateful for being alive. The next three rounds will be of a different chemical combo, so who knows what is coming, for better or worse! I'm grateful for Richard's keeping the household going and giving me space and support. Pain and gratitude can co-exist, I am learning.

Dear ones:

I honestly felt puny until day 16 of this cycle. On the five days of feeling relatively good I celebrated by being in the kitchen. My reduced physical activity along with increased calories from what the nutritionist recommends has resulted in my putting a pound back on, which made the oncologist smile today.

Richard was in bed with stomach flu for three days. (Ah, yes, when one's immune system is most vulnerable, here comes the threat from inside the house. So much for the illusion of control!) But last evening he got up and participated in a ritual that felt important for us. I colored some water red-orange to match the 'dragon juice' of the first three rounds of chemo cocktails I just finished. Also on the tray I had a glass of clear water, to represent the upcoming new drug.

We stood in our backyard and each in our own words thanked the dragon juice for stepping up to do the heavy lifting, while we poured it out onto the ground. We toasted the new drug with the glass of clear water, affirming its healthful purpose, and pledging our support for its turn at bat. My continuing prayer is for my body to cooperate with the chemical warfare: to be able to do its part to take in the agent and allow it to work efficiently, then rebound toward vibrance, however small the step. So as we finished our ritual to mark a new change, we cried at the power of it—feeling united, peaceful, grateful.

One half of chemo ends, opening a new round of unknown.

love, amy

Five
Breathing Free

I left for lab work at 10:15 a.m. Taking photos of my oncology team for my journal was fun; receiving the results of blood work, not. White cells plummeted. Red cells maintained the low, low level of last cycle. Platelets fell further. The numbers fit with how puny I have felt this cycle, but the news knocked the wind out of my sails.

Fear sat on my shoulder in the examining room, hurling questions and doubts: *Is this going in the wrong direction? Why the dramatic shift? Do I dare feel good that my red counts did not go even lower? Does this mean postponing further chemo? Is this to be expected? What can I expect? I am only halfway through my cycles—can I make it the rest of the way? Will I be strong enough? How do I trust my body, when it is so weary and struggling?*

It's so hard to know whether to have expectations — high or low. What seems to be at risk is hope. The danger in expecting any straight-line positive trajectory is a fragile sense of peace. The oncologist walked in and sat with my questions, the ones I was brave enough to voice. He told me that the white counts should come back up, but there is nothing I can do to increase them.

Surrender always has been hard for me. I breathe. I breathe.

~~~

Not surprisingly, I felt agitated tonight. I can't multitask anymore without consequence. I burn dinner. I loose track. I'm concerned about whether cognitive damage from chemo will be long lasting. *Can I be gentle with myself about this, with this, through this?*

I try to stay positive, but everything seems to require new effort. Going to the bathroom, not being able to go. Making dinner, not wanting to eat. Perpetually wondering what choice will be good for me or affect me adversely. *Is this mindfulness or madness—observing with such care, attention, detail?* Over-focusing is not the antidote to denial.

I took out a recent photo of a sunflower and saw the seeds in its dark center. I reminded myself that this center is also ringed by light. Tonight, though, darkness needs to speak.

Finding Strength in Vulnerability

This period of churning seems to overwhelm my best intentions to find my calm courage. I decided to give voice to the pain and fear, to pour it all out in a letter to God.

Dear God,

This morning I offer you this mess of a mind: swirling confusion, not-sure what-is-what anymore, all the fits and starts of being a pilgrim at healing.

I am tired today of being the warrior—is there not another way? Couldn't I trade warrior for bluebird? Does even asking this show a lack of courage on my part?

Each day I struggle with all there is to do and learn and choose from, just to heal.

God, give me the strength to:

walk, stretch, strengthen, practice yoga, move, dance, laugh, cook, eat, supplement, read, write, connect, update, respond, give back, love Richard, brush teeth, listen, love myself, pray, meditate, visualize, show up for therapy, clean, monitor, calm, observe, think, not think, refrain, immerse, ask, question, declare, trust.

And that's the easy stuff.

Help me choose well, with ease, and stay
the course, forgiving myself when I forget to eat
my broccoli or take my pills on time, or lose my
bearings in a parking lot, again.

Help me navigate the tougher stuff with grace.
Tougher stuff like figuring how to detach and
attach at the same time, letting go in a way
that says I very much still want to live.

My plans now replaced by a mystery I say yes
to, with a quiver in my voice.

Wobbly from chemo I now meet myself on a
new precipice. Meet me there. Better yet, help
me remember that You are there before me,
waiting to hold me close.
Amen.

~~~

Through this cycle of treatment, all I could do was lie flat or sit, and read and pray, for days. A week of nose bleeds, dizzy, swollen, cotton-mouthed, weak-legged. Only sitting provided relief.

With sight still partially blurred, I slowly absorbed *The Book Thief*. Timely. Yes, words can destroy or heal. Art and hope are inextricably linked. Love can make all the difference. I felt like I was reading my way back to life as I resonated with the characters.

This week, when I finally could sit up long enough, I wrote. It was cathartic. Unable to sleep, I sat in the dark in front of my computer screen and poured out my restlessness.

Tongue nuzzles my teeth
for a chance to feel potent.
Tastebuds and more flinch
on their pasty surface,
sacrificing themselves
like fine-grained sandpaper
on a mission,
worn down, nearly numb,
to make a swallow smooth.

Tongue swollen white
hard to look at
like a discovered porpoise
lolling on Irish beach,
a few signs of pink
around the edges
signal hope.

All muscles,
bones, joints
and all other parts of living
ache.
How can the moon through my window
give enough light to draw dreams by?
There is rest, blessed rest.
There is morning light to pray by,
or to count the new red spots on my arms
scattered like confetti
over a parade of trust.

Fingers can't touch fingers
toes can't touch shoes
all painful after
yesterday's chemical strafe.
Nails now indigo streams
of morse code
call all cells to stations.
What stands as triumph
knowing war is hell?

After days of dull fatigue and frustration about my worsening mental changes, I pray for the patience to wait this through. I haven't known myself forgetting so much. I scramble thoughts. I misspell words. I spell words backwards. Putting more than one sentence together often can take more energy than I have. Sometimes it takes a half hour to write a paragraph. But I write anyway. I can recall and order the words better if I write than speak.

I am not the only one to notice. People see firsthand my inability to engage and they try to help fill in the gaps, making the gaps all the more prominent to me. They guess what I am intending as I have to point to a zipper instead of naming it. They wait an eternity for the right word to hit the tip of my tongue.

It tires me now to follow conversations, requiring my brain to be so focused. I don't want many people around, seeing me like this. My mind had generally been more like a steel trap than a sieve; my competence, always my bedrock. In failing to retrieve my words, I feel like I am losing ground, unable to retrieve myself. A huge gap between how I was and how I am now.

Who will come out the other side of this? Hold me steady, God.

Healing with Love

Fortunately, I had a lifeline in my friend who guides my visualizations. And I had the energy to call her. I mustered the courage to have her hear my trouble with words.

She welcomed my call and began by leading me to imagine a safe place for healing. I saw myself sit on a rock in the stream below our last house. I leaned against the mossy creek bank, splashes of water and leftover leaves tickling the smaller rocks at my feet. The air, chilly and fresh, paired well with the sun, warming my face. After a time of breathing into these sensations, a Christ figure in a light hooded robe with a gentle face stood beside me, radiating peace. I experienced no agenda from him, no push, just his ease in approaching me, offering comfort. In the silence inside myself, I asked his name: "*I am Love.*" He enfolded me, rocked me; all of me felt safe, warm. "*Focus on me and you will find yourself; this calm peaceful moment is real.*"

My body felt the truth of it for a long while, until another question rose from my heart, not my out-of-kilter brain: *How do I love myself?* Again, from the well of silence came this message: "*Start from your heart. See yourself through my eyes, the eyes of the heart. You have done so with others, clear-sighted about their wholeness. Don't let the deep healing work get lost in the shuffle of the day. You know what to do.*"

At the end of the visualization, my friend and I discussed how the heart welcomes any gap as a new way of being, whereas the mind makes comparisons, judges it as less. For now, at least, my usual analytical mode of expression is giving way to a more intuitive one. Mind is invited to step aside to let heart lead.

I felt directly today how Love would cradle me across the threshold.

A month later…

I hated saying goodbye to my stepfather today. His visit brought great joy even as I prepared for a chemo treatment. Before leaving, he walked into the kitchen and surprised me with a gift — a garment he bought for himself decades before I knew him, at a market in Morocco. He explained that this djellaba was worn over clothes to protect the wearer from the blazing sun and stinging sand of the desert. He offered: "I didn't need to keep this in my closet; you might appreciate this now." Speechless, I accepted the gift.

I was stunned at the synchronicity. This resembled the robe in my visualization, gauzy and white, but with gold embroidery around the neck. *How could this be*? Only my private journal knew that story. *The Spirit at work*, I mused silently as I tried it on, seeing how perfectly it fit.

~~~

I put in my journal these words by Christine Paintner: "Hope is a stance of radical openness to the God of newness and possibility. When we hope, we acknowledge that God has an imagination far more expansive than ours."

No coincidences.

Dear ones:

Halfway through cycle four, it's been a different ride, better and worse than the previous ones. Today I went for lab work, usual for this point, and for the first time in four cycles, the white and red blood counts maintained! How do I explain the good results? My best guess is that it's the first day of June and we need rain! It's about that rational or predictable.

The first part of the cycle, on steroids to offset the effects of this new chemo drug, I had energy galore, no sense of having had a treatment, no nausea, hungry even. I kept my ambition focused on touching up some wall paint, and reorganizing part of the kitchen to make room for a new water treatment system that will remove impurities from tap water—another act to reduce recurrence. After the steroid wore off, it took me over a week to feel my tongue (with or without ulcers). Digestive plagues and body aches hit. One day I literally woke up not able to touch my finger or toenails; that sensitivity lasted for days. Richard had to open the cereal box; I couldn't hold a pen. The change was dramatic, overnight, scary. I had assumed that one chemo drug rather than the former cocktail of three would be easier. Not so.

I now have early swelling with lymphedema, and per a physical therapy specialist, I'll need to wear a compression sleeve when exercising. I ordered it in rose, reminding me to live "in the pink"! And, we bought a mini-trampoline for helping with lymph flow. Ah, the whirl of this — one day I can't hold a pen, and days later am planning for exercise. Good thing I've learned how healthy belly laughter can be for my lymph system.

Gentleness is the watchword these days. So easy to be tempted to say 'yes' to more after the body has been laboring under 'no' for so long.

After my lab tests today I purposely went to Brookgreen Gardens to take a few photos to mark the change to summer flowers, and to let my mind and heart open to the beauty and peacefulness there. Passing a couple, I overheard the words, "...a synthesis she could live with." These being the only words I heard on my walk, I smiled at how perfect and relevant. As I walked, then paused, a powder blue dragonfly landed on a reed next to the water lily I was photographing. It perched, stayed. I moved and clicked the shutter. It stayed. I sat. Its presence reminded me that I can pause like this, freely.

These days of trial that are so hard on my body but so rich for my spirit call me to find a "synthesis I can live with." **What is the 'now-this' that comes after living through 'what-was,' and 'what-is-no-longer'?** To me, it means having the courage to live well by being emptied and opened, not despite that. To accept being thrown off the horse and made blind in order to see differently. To be patient with my own fumbling and doubt. God knows, this is work.

love, amy

~~~

A dear colleague wrote me today after reading my latest update: "I am holding my breath for you."

"Please don't hold your breath. Breathe WITH me!" I responded.

~~~

And a former client wrote:

Your body is under attack and your mind is capturing it and recording it for the future. When you emerge on the other side of this, changed forever in some ways, you will be whom you essentially have always been. You will use your writing to describe new horizons for some, or define places you want to explore or return to. As your body takes care of the serious business at hand, breathe. Have no fear.

I responded:

Your words, my dear, so powerful, wise, fill me. It IS a bit ridiculous to assume I should be feeling great when under attack. Thanks for the reminders to be gentle with myself. I think about POWs who never know if they will be released. At least I have a schedule for when my treatments end. Truly, I never know when or if this disease might recur. This too feels like indefinite capture some days. But aren't

we all living under the Sword of Damocles
every moment? I will not let the question of
how long I have dominate how I live my life.
Breathe with me.

~~~

Richard shared with me an email he sent a dear friend, describing me as steady. I am grateful for these glimpses of myself, through his loving eyes.

You've asked about how Amy's doing, overall.
I give her a 10, except for occasional dives to
a 5 or 7 or 2 when the chemo poison is doing
a number on her G.I. tract. Those dives last
from half an hour to a day. She reminds me of
the inflatable punching bag a friend sent her.
You can smack it very hard and it flips itself
upright. Physically, she is doing about as well
as could be expected: no terrible surprises
as of now. Emotionally, she is holding steady
like a clipper in a tempest. Spiritually, she is
stronger than ever. Connected and centered.
I look forward to a few more decades with her
re-forged life force.

Giving The Signs Room to Speak

This morning I found myself at an amusement park standing at the base of a huge roller coaster, designed by a German man. I looked up and couldn't see the top of it. The tallest loop reached to the sky, and behind it I could see the Milky Way in the dark. I was astonished. The coaster was called "*Teleheileid*," spelled out clearly on the sign. Just as I read the word, I woke up from this very vivid dream.

After a bit more waking up, I decided to investigate any possible meaning to this dream and the title of the coaster. I researched the word *teleos*, signifying end or purpose. A teleological argument supports the existence of God, implying that there is a divine directive principle at work. Then I looked up *heil* and found that it meant healthy. And *leid* meant suffering. So I sat and played with these meanings: *healthy suffering that serves a purpose designed by God.* What a dream! What a ride I am living!

Dear ones:

I find moments of this cancer journey miraculous.

When I went into the oncologist's office this morning to get blood drawn to determine IF my counts were high enough to receive treatment, the results floored me: **These can't be my numbers. Are you sure you have the right person?** White counts that were off-the-scale low 10 days ago were now at the top of the range; the swing, dramatic. Red counts went up to earlier levels. Platelets rose significantly.

The oncologist, surprised, explained that perhaps the injections taken each cycle to boost the counts reached a critical threshold, and finally kicked in. Of course I wanted to know what specifically to attribute this to, so it could be replicated. Then I sat back, remarking at the mystery of it all, the grace of resiliency. My body did this!! I accept that I won't be able to know why this big a shift for the good happened; I expect there was some benefit from all the levels of help my body was given — chemical, spiritual, nutritional, mental, relational. But I'll take the news and rejoice. I'm careful not to assume that this will be the case through the last two cycles. Mystery works its own sweet pattern.

Several experiences last week kept me mindful of signs along the way. A friend sent me a Bozo the Clown punching bag. I remember these from childhood; never had one, always wanted one. She had suggested that this period of being knocked down and coming back up could be symbolized by this "schmoo," and it might do me good to punch it now and then.

So I blew it up, and punched it, gently at first, like a three or four year old might. It did what it was supposed to do: went down; came back up for more. Several times. Then I punched it harder. Adult rage, chemo strength! And it fell over, lying on its side, not getting back up without my help. Ugh. I didn't need this kind of image: knocked flat. I propped it in the corner of the room, where at least it could make me smile, and I avoided any more punching.

On my first day of feeling good this cycle, I decided to take Bozo out of the corner and blow more air into him. I realized, as I filled this vinyl funny man, that I was breathing more deeply in the process. Long, slow, deep inhales and exhales, and resting, until he could hold no more. All his crevices filled in. And I checked and reshaped the sand ballast, making sure it was centered and balanced on the figure. Then wham! I gave it a real punch. And he came through. Down and up. Down and up. He sustained several good strong hits, coming back to face me, as if on a dare. I laughed. All he needed was more breath in him, a good balance to assure footing, and another chance! Of course, the meaning was not lost on me.

Each day I attend more to my own breath work, and tune in to how to reshape the 'sand' at my base to keep standing, even in my surreal world of minimal activity. I have sacrificed dinners out, activities with friends and family when it feels like too much, said no to a planned trip with Richard to the North Carolina mountains. I write more. I pray more. I exert less.

Relative to lymphedema symptoms, I will begin exercises with the specialist next week to nudge the lymph fluid to where my body can reabsorb it better. Unknowingly, I had been doing my own massaging in the wrong direction — toward my hands. A dear friend, trained as a physical therapist, offered this to me: "It's the return of the lymph that's difficult. Once it goes to the hands, it needs to move; the object is to get it back to the **heart**." I stopped her mid-explanation and asked her to repeat her words. I needed to pause to take in this message fully. It echoed the meditation that started my day: "Make us know the shortness of our life, that we may gain wisdom of heart." (Psalm 90:12)

So much is speaking now. Perhaps to listen is the invitation — the necessary, critical, faithful response. Thanks for being with me in so many wonderful ways. Pray for all who are suffering in whatever way.

love, amy

Six
Light to Make the Turns

Dear ones:

Your various and abundant expressions
of love have been and are sources of
healing balm. Bountiful prayers, stories,
encouragement, clarity, perspective,
feedback, and laughter, all treasures. I am
overwhelmed at your offering of yourselves,
speechless most days.

I am humbled by the impact. I map my
journey, and you report your changes for
the good that my changes seem to catalyze.
I am moved by the power of connection:
my words and your words comingle, ripple
in concentric circles beyond ourselves. How
can this not be a factor in my healing?
I will continue to seek the meaning that
is unfolding in all this, and to share my
learning with you, even as I am learning
from you.

love, amy

~~~

The Laughter Club meeting at the library teaches me that different breaths and vocal sounds exercise different body organs. What a hoot to practice as a group! I give thanks for the giggle grams a friend made these last many weeks, the box of hilarious videos another sent. Humor was relegated to the back seat for much of my professional drive. Now I can see it at least slipping into the passenger seat!

At today's meditation class — such a contrast with the laughter, or maybe not so very different. Breath heals.

With only four of us there, we sat together in silence for a half hour, listening to the pouring rain. I kept watching thoughts come and go. For a few minutes, I was able to experience that pure space of no-thought. Like undulating breath, in, out. A sense of endlessness, beyond words. For a few minutes, I felt like I was all breath and yet not aware of breathing. Still and moving. Utter peace.

And then it passed, and my mind raced off to wonder whether I am focusing on the right things to heal. I prayed for all those suffering, in whatever form, and for ease within my own restless mind. *Ah, what ground gets covered in a half hour.*

Welcoming a New Incarnation

My email to a friend:

All body hair is gone. Nothing prepares you to see your eyes without brows or lashes for the first time. By now my utter baldness surprises only those who come to the door, unawares. Richard daily kisses my head, tenderly. The peach fuzz that is starting to grow seems like early crocus. It signals a chapter change. So easily I turn to questions: What will I look like with hair again? Will I like the new me? Will I miss this simple ease? Gratitude sometimes has to work up nerve on a winding path.

Today on my walk, an epiphany. I realized that when I look in the mirror I am able to see my head as maybe only my parents or God had ever seen it. To have this experience of baldness is like being let in on a most intimate sight. I could imagine myself in that earlier form, innocent, beloved, newly born. A lot of mileage today with that gestalt!

After I finished writing it, I noticed that it is becoming easier to share what would have been reserved for my personal journal.

~~~

A former client stunned me with his openness today. His unexpected email, responding to one of my updates, was filled with reflection on his own cancer experience. He offered me his lessons learned:

> *Priorities become clearer. Sharing stories connect us as fellow travelers. A deeper life purpose forms. Pleasure gets redefined. Peripheral vision gets reset, never to go back to what it was.*

I sat for a while, then wrote him back:

> *I am learning more about what this rite of passage is about. There is a softening happening in me, both in my physical practice of yoga and in my way of viewing the world. My DO beast is learning to lie next to the lamb. But relaxing into ambiguity is a real piece of work for me. I cannot plan or control where all this ends. I now need to see myself as a good book unfolding, page after page. I can't just jump ahead to the last paragraph.*
>
> *Victorious seems to mean staying the course, and believing that no matter where I end up, that is the right place. Along the way, moments are magnificent, terrifying, peace-giving. So much depends on the lens I am using at the time, and whether my mind or heart dominates its shape.*

I was surprised that I would admit this to a man who lives and leads like a drink out of a fire hose. But courage begets courage.

Another former client, living with metastasized breast cancer that continues to defy odds year after year, called today. She opened up to me:

> *I feel life slipping out of control. I had always found ways to live around and through, using shortcuts even, and always made it, just-in-time, even if were just before the gun went off and the race started. Living in control. This time I can't. I was always counted on to keep commitments. Now I see that my assumption of control brought on too many of those commitments.*

We talked about redefining what one can control. The thought popped into my head: *Amazing how when we define our own situation as different, we forget to look and listen to what we already deeply know. She needed to be reminded to apply her own wisdom.* So I suggested: "Create a space for you, much like you advised me at diagnosis to be ruthless about setting boundaries, to protect space to heal."

"You mean I can DO that??" She paused. "I was never taught how to do less. Doing more has always been an important anchor to get me through."

We both let silence bless our mutual confession.

Then I recapped a lesson from my priest's recent sermon: "In a roiling storm threatening to capsize our boat, we hold onto anchors, even beloved ones, at our peril." We agreed: this path to healing is not as straight as we thought, and requires the courageous giving up of what no longer stabilizes us.

~~~

A wise friend called today to ask how I was doing. As I described all the parts of me undergoing change, he described it as a "new incarnation." He offered, "It's a choice how we look at aspects of a former life and how we label the contrast with what is currently the case. It takes courage, and a change of view, to get to a place of gratitude." I'll admit to many years of running hard, tuning in more to the call of the wild ego than to centering prayer, taking way too much for granted.

Today is Pentecost. Although incarnation might be more apropos of Christmas than this holy day, I understand now how walking out of that Upper Room to a new life took a courage that had to feel like fire.

~~~

Spent all day with my sister-in-law who lives nearby to sew the quilt for my granddaughter to come. I loved the quiet ease of the day, the work, the careful attending to details. Talking or not. With each knot tied, a prayer: "Bless this child." A simple lunch on her screened porch.

I returned home to a FedEx box containing an amazing gift from several alumni representing the leadership course I led with colleagues over the years. (The one in which I used the falling leaf image to illustrate transition). They created a lap quilt to look like a big picture window, with each of several unique panes bordered with hearts. Each contributor selected an image that mattered to him or her: a bouquet of flowers, a sunset, a poem, a prayer, a symbol of the work we did together, a photo of the group, an empty pocket as if waiting for things to come. I sobbed, speechless. At the art of it. At the self-revealing and care in the design. At the time and effort to put it together. At this work of love.

I immediately called my sister-in-law to come see it. Moved, she asked, "How long did you work with these people?" "A total of six days, over a year," I said. We sat for many minutes in silence, incredulous. How is it that in such a short amount of time we can touch others' lives so deeply? In those courses, I gave what I could. I grew, too. And now this taste of heaven. Abundance indeed!

A couple days later, I sat down and wrote my letter of thanks to my quilt designers. This time, words just flowed out of me.

Friends,

How inadequate my expression of gratitude for your love, prayerful support, and incredible creative energy. What you came together to produce, despite your hugely busy days, and the complexity of the art form itself, is clearly above and beyond. I so appreciate how you honored our past work together —the work YOU did; I was only the instrument.

I find in this quilt the miracle of how people connect through vulnerability. As a human community, we are like a quilt bordered in hearts, the seams strong when love is the basis for our work in the world.

I can envision your faces before me. Amazing that months and years can pass and we can still resurrect those powerful moments that invited us to become more awake. And to lead from there.

Together we risked taking off our comfortable masks and shaking up the routine of our lives, to make way for truths that needed to emerge. So I am calling this my resurrection quilt, sewn with memories that are life giving. I sit at the foot of this healing process and learn what the new incarnation asks of me.

Thank you. From the bottom of my heart, and the top of my bald head, and all the rest of me that is making its way through, thank you. Some of you who have walked a similar path know the power of support. All of us walk a way that takes twists and turns, and calls for transformation when we least expect. So, we hold our lanterns high together, even when our arms hurt. We pray together. And that's the way we know hope in the depths of our souls.

Bless you, as you are blessing me.

Amy

Keeping Vigil

My first granddaughter is due today! Going through this day-as-vigil helps me notice more intently the measure of moments. I imagine what our pregnant daughter across the country is bearing at this hour. As I picked up my prescription earlier this morning—the pharmacist knows me by name now—I heard the in-store music. (I've learned more about how to wait and listen.) "I Hope You Dance" sounded over the speaker — the song she danced with her father at her wedding, and one of my favorites. I can't help but notice the timing. I smiled all the way to the oncologist's office for my shot to boost my blood count.

As I sit, my favorite nurse comes in, seven months pregnant. Of course we talk about the expecting, the pending births. We promise to pray, to call each other with news. As I leave the office and walk to my car, the bumper sticker on the car next to mine heralds, "Grace Happens." *Faith is such a mysterious adventure.*

~~~

Vigil time can be a gift. Awake, wondering through the night, I was trying not to worry, at 1:11, 2:15, 3:08, 4:15, 5:30. At 5:45 a.m. I got up, and prayed, "All is possible with God." I felt the shift, the lift, and I left the house for a walk. To have enough energy to walk is not a given, so I was grateful for what I had today.

When I returned in less than an hour, Richard was beaming. "We have news!" He relayed every detail, lovingly. I could visualize her dark hair and heather eyes, all six pounds 13 ounces, 17.5 inches of her! It wasn't lost on me that just when I acted in accord with my own healing, the news I awaited arrived.

A few hours later I sat in my sunroom to finish hemming the baby quilt. Richard walked in with the first picture of our OHHHhhhlivia! emailed from a camera phone. *How can she ever know how important she has been for so many months already, how she inspired me through treatments? How can she know that her months of gestation will mirror my own — from diagnosis to end of radiation? And now she is here with a strong start to a new life, as I am committing to mine.* Today I am writing all this so one day she can see some of this life through my eyes.

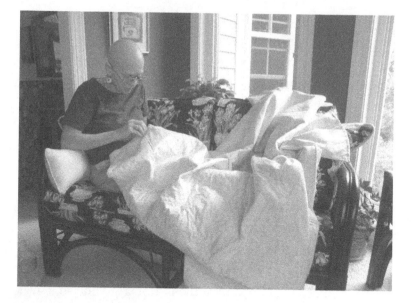

Letting Pain Speak

I usually note in my journal the particulars of pain, so I can track any changes or patterns to report to my oncologist. I decide how much I want to share more publicly.

Tonight, pain's voice is demanding, relentless. I surrender. Maybe if I write through the pain, it will calm down. Or at least I might relax even if the spasms don't, by focusing differently, by getting out of bed. I'm learning to breathe through the crescendo of pain and write at the same time. I sit with the blank screen before me, eyes closed, waiting. Words come. It doesn't matter how good the work; I'm writing to remember and release. How suffering and inspiration mingle inside me. What a pair!

Six days of steroid
keep symptoms and sleep
at bay,
then lay down the armor,
meeting full-faced the
remnants of the night.
Labored breath, raging
against a cage of ribs
swell and release
like an ocean swallowed,
relentless.
All my heart can do is
pound its hope.

Waiting for the wave of
cramps to pass
involuntary whimper rises
from the bowels:
my personal wailing wall.
A surrendered moan,
resisting restraint,
its own kind of prayer.
An outcry ends the
nightmare. I waken from
shadow
shaken and relieved,
tears on my cheek the only
sign of terror's visit.

Eyes out of sync,
blurred, prismatic.
Effort to see requires focus at a slant—
the not-usual now being the way.
To expect image without distortion
is distortion.
To make effortless the adjustment,
new way opens.

Gums heed the unwelcome call to retreat.
Failing to reform the line
loyally held these fifty-odd years,
sad they must be, to lose their place.
Tooth after tooth breaks down in the melee,
attention no longer a stand they can take.
Some battles are just too much.

Mouth masquerades as cotton
blooming in the heat
despite impoverished soil,
waiting for water
despite the drought.
Faith hangs tough,
rising up like wilting stalks of pink hydrangeas
defying the summer scorch.

~~~

The next morning, I awoke remembering a dream. A small androgynous character walked up to me and asked, "Why are you not working or traveling now? Are you choosing frail?" *No*, I replied, *I am choosing spiritual*. The character looked at me then faded away.

Later, I wrote to a client, describing that dream: "You might think I am going crazy as I tell you this, but it's amazing what is being opened as I give myself time to rest, breathe, pray and take in the moment. That is a work of its own. I wish you joy and peace as you discover your true rhythm."

Dear ones:

I am learning in bold about grief and pain. About being patient with the twists and turns of this process. About willing myself to stay in the game during the in-from-left-field challenges. About facing up to impermanence. It all changes: what I depend on for support; the effects of treatment cycles; my attachment to life as I have known it or imagine it should be. I try to stare down the expectations that spike fear—thinking I should be here or there, that this should or shouldn't be the case, that it's my job to find the rhyme or reason or discernible pattern to things I essentially can't control.

So many opposites to reconcile. I need to be proactive without fatiguing myself with effort. I want to attend to real needs without obsessing. I want to hang on to signs of hope while the signs keep changing.

I commit to saving my life while knowing my limitations in that purpose. Humbling to realize what I can and cannot do and the self-forgiveness that requires. So much loving support buoys my trust that all will be well, even as my body struggles to fight the good fight.

Spiritually this time is one of the richest of my life. Each week I am learning more about surrender as layer after layer of expectation is being peeled away. I am getting accustomed to sleeplessness as a time to have good heart-to-hearts with God. As my body is brought low — being emptied in a way, my spirit is getting clearer about what in me matters, what is timeless and pure. I am seeing now that emptied and lighter will be the new page for whatever future is writing itself.

love, amy

Carrying Light Forward

I shared with my therapist today my impatience, fear, and grief in the midst of all this not-knowing. It's not clear what I can count on, if that means counting on it not to change. In the face of hearing from my medical oncologist, "There is nothing you can do" about my plummeting blood counts, I still have expectations. Of course the biggest fear — *Will I make it through this?* — steals my breath, again and again.

My therapist listens. She offers the image of me being both the carrier of light, and light itself: "You are making powerful shifts spiritually, transitioning and transforming, and your body is doing the same, even if it feels weak." She suggested leading a Peaceful Dying meditation to focus on impermanence. She wanted to help me strengthen my capacity to be present with fear, while detaching from trying to control how a day unfolds. I felt an initial clutch of resistance, heart-thumping fear at facing the ultimate fear. But I decided, in her care, to trust the process.

She began with an invitation: imagining a special place. People. Memory after memory came into view. Sitting with Richard in the wild rose and blackberry fields in Mendocino where we were married. Walking in our woods. Cooking school in Umbria with mom. Laughter. Work I loved. Faces of family members, friends, colleagues. More.

As I held all these clearly in mind, she asked me what I needed to say, bless, forgive, or finish with these loved ones. I breathed. I saw each face one by one and imagined the exchange; I could hear the words as tears actually soaked my shirt. After a while, a sense of incredible gratitude for their lives replaced my pain.

Then she instructed me to turn away from them and find and enter a spaciousness bigger than I could imagine imagining. After a few minutes of silence and deep breathing, I was able to see myself turn toward an expansive dark blue space that filled my whole being, heart, lungs. In the distance, a light. I turned around to see Richard, family, and I cry my resistance, not wanting to go. A friend appears and offered to be my midwife, to help me make the turn. One last time facing the void, I take a few steps. Appearing before me, many faces: mom, dad, other loved ones who had died, others who were part of my life, some whom I didn't recognize. My cousin, who recently died from cancer, comes up to me, radiant, calm. She is clothed in a light garment, the color of a yellow peach. When she takes my hand and leads me toward the light, faces are lining each side of a channel-like path. I am taken into this image, and I have no fear. I no longer feel any inclination to turn back.

After a long silence to let the power of this settle...

My therapist asked a few more questions. One in particular touched a new truth: "What enabled you to turn?" I answered: *The fullness of the space, its peace, light.* She asked how this might translate to the present time in my life: "What does the God in you say to you now?" I spoke aloud the words speaking through me: *Stay the course. You will find peace. I've got you.*

I experienced a feeling of courage and peace I had not thought possible.

I took several minutes to make notes in my journal. We ended the session with an affirmation I could carry with me: **I commit to this path, knowing I am fully supported by Divine Love. I can accept the real impermanence of this life, and commit to live each moment.**

I know now I have what I need to make the turn to the light.

Inspiration to Thrive

With blood counts good after my fifth chemo treatment, the oncologist approved my attending a free conference at Furman University: "Cancer as a Turning Point—from Surviving to Thriving." I had received an invitation in the mail just a week after my lumpectomy. Intrigued, pulled to attend, I registered the next day, and kept the brochure in plain sight even though I had no idea what the crystal ball held.

Richard readily agreed to accompany me, checking off his space on the registration form, "Family Caregiver/ Support." We drove the five hours, grateful for a first weekend away in six months, a unique celebration for our wedding anniversary. *Ah the grace of doing something that feels normal.*

Over 600 cancer survivors filled the auditorium: couples of all ages, women with sisters or friends, many arriving solo. Most had hair, so I felt a bit self-conscious in my baldness. Outrageous tropical earrings helped. The conference opened with a flutist on stage. She finished her prelude, and the program moderator — herself a breast cancer survivor eight times over — introduced the weekend.

She asked people to stand as a particular category described them. She started with calling out "Survivor" and although many were getting to their feet, I stayed sitting. I thought I couldn't claim this until some time in the future, after all treatments, after some kind of permanent all-clear. She then clarified: "If you are currently in treatment and wondering if you fit this category — you are a survivor if you are here today." Many more of us, me included, stood then, and the applause began. My legs wobbled, my throat choked with emotion as I, for the first time, felt the truth of this from inside out: *Yes, right now, I AM here!* Richard sat beside me with his arm around my waist, and it was one of the most glorious moments of my life.

For two days, we were inspired to heal smartly and celebrate life. Singers, authors, composers, doctors, nutritionists, dancers, musicians, and storytellers gifted us with their wisdom and energy, admitting how their lives had been transformed by the very disease that brought us all together. We were encouraged to explore various healing modalities: guided imagery; nutritional, spiritual and psychological support; music; movement and exercise; laughter. I felt affirmed in my own discovery of these and learned new things as well. Richard and I stood side by side in guided yoga stretches. We sat moved by performances that unfolded a picture of a treacherous path and graceful passage. We sang. We laughed. We cried. We listened. This liturgy, gentle and strong, professed surviving as an opportunity, while recognizing that not all before us would be easy.

At one point, I volunteered to go onstage with others to experience Japanese taiko drumming for the first time. I felt my arms dance strong against the drum, and then lift high, heart pounding its own beat of hope. To choose to live full-out, without putting brakes on my heart's desire; to know clearly that life is short and best-laid plans can be upstaged in a blink were truths worth drumming into my head and heart. And that I did.

As we stood to leave the auditorium, I motioned over to our seats an amazing actress walking out before us. She had staged a one-woman masterpiece, depicting her own recurring rounds of treatments. Her portrayal made me howl with laughter, nod my knowing, wince, and sob. "Thank you, thank you for showing me what can come on the other side," I whispered to her: "You are a gift to the world." She hugged me close, her full head of curly hair brushing my baldness. She moved in from the aisle to stand beside Richard, honoring my request for a picture of them together. I noticed that as I was putting my camera away, she spoke briefly to him.

On the walk back to the car I asked what she said to him in parting. "She told me she had been sitting a couple rows behind us during some of the performances, watching me rub your head. She said it touched her to see so much love." We both went silent. Then he added, "I heard her words and thought, 'I had this impact on *her*? I was merely doing what felt good to *me*.'"

That drive home that seemed not-so-long was filled with our telling and retelling the story of the weekend. We were not the same couple of three days ago. We wondered out loud what *our* emerging on the other side of all this would look like. Without saying another word, we signed on to finding out.

~~~

The following Saturday, four days before my last chemo, Richard and I took a drive.

While I was buying pink lady black-eyed peas at the outdoor Farmers' Market, a man walked up to me and asked, "Are you a cancer survivor?" He must have noticed my hairlessness. "Yes," I answered.

95

He, too, one of us, throat cancer. He went through 42 radiation treatments. I tell him that I'm just about to start my 30. "Good luck. Hang in there. Bless you, " he encouraged. We clasped hands. Eyes teared up at the immediate bond. Glad I was not wearing my floppy hat today, so he could recognize me, a fellow survivor. I thought to myself, *SURVIVOR, yes, I said it easily today.*

Dear ones:

I am officially declaring today my independence day. CHEMO IS FINISHED! Richard accompanied me to this last treatment; it felt right to end this chapter together.

And my hair is starting to grow back. I am taking bets now on what color and texture will finally emerge from the fuzz. I'm actually going to miss the ease of this bald look. No bad hair day.

Next steps? We are waiting for a consult with the radiation oncologist, after another ultrasound to make sure he is working from the most current picture. Richard and I are also researching the post-chemo medication options I will take for the foreseeable future.

So, I THANK YOU, for your care, contact, prayers during these months. Here's to a new beginning, this time in a lead-lined room. I know the difference you have made for me, through the grace of God. You are the fireworks in my sky!

love, amy

Seven
Land In-Between

Richard and I cancel plans for Friday night, the getaway weekend trip we paid for a year ago. I can't travel light so easily now with all the meds and supports I need to sleep and eat well. The decision seems the right one. It feels freeing to see this space as opportunity without feeling compelled to say yes, just because we made a plan. Seems like lots of deposits are being lost these months.

My new metric now for deciding what to take on: *Think this through. Is this activity the right thing at this time? What toll is associated with this? Does it feel light or heavy? What is the gain if I say yes, if I say no?*

Healing in Full Color

My intention for today's visualization by phone: *What does healing look like?* After the stillness and breath work, I imagine myself sitting in a beige room, reaching up as if painting the walls: first the bright red of watermelon, then deep blue, spring green. My room becomes a canvas large enough to walk in. Then I see the colors inside me, swirling, swirling. My arms are actually buzzing and my

97

hands are actually warm. I see myself walking with these rays of colored light coming out of me, outlining my body and extending out several feet, out of my room, into the landscape around me. As I walk, I stop at a stream, look into it, and see my reflection. The color coming from me is not like a mask, it is truly me! I see my shape fade, and all that is left are my eyes and these colors. The water takes on the colors, and I feel the warmth of the sun over my left shoulder as I continue to marvel at the reflection. I hear myself give thanks.

Moving back from the water in a sun salutation—an awakening movement I learned in yoga — I hear: *Live boldly. Shine as I do, even on the dark days.* I vow to remember.

As the visualization ends, I feel calm, warm. The picture of those colors emanating from my body, still vivid.

We finished the call. I immediately sat and made notes in my journal about the experience. As I finished, the doorbell rang. A woman stood in the doorway bearing a bouquet of colored balloons, in a small beige vase decorated with a sunflower. Manifesting before me were the same colors in my visualization!

I called my friend who guided the process to tell her what had just occurred, but mainly to hear myself claim this synchronicity. "Live your colors; that is the healing!" she affirmed. Then I called the friend living many states away who sent the bouquet. The message on the card: "I am right next door!" I could imagine her shaking her head in amazement, as I did, about the happening of this day.

What other signs are right next to me, waiting for me to see?

In the waiting period between chemo and radiation, my body, like a good bread dough, is given time to rest before asking it to rise...

Richard and I went together for my lab work. All results good. We stopped at the wallpaper store just to browse. Time to redo my office, finally. As we walked aisle by aisle, looking for an appealing print, I finally spotted a candidate — beige background with dusty-miller-blue dragonflies! I wanted something light, to allow the art pieces to pop. And I wanted something to remind me of easy summer moments with my niece, sitting and spitting watermelon seeds into the pond out back, dragonflies circling our toes.

For years they have delighted me; they fly around me often, about anywhere. Last week, a friend told the story of how a dragonfly was once a dragon but now a messenger to offer light through change.

We asked for a sample of that wallpaper.

Later, in researching dragonflies, for the fun of it, I learned more. Dragonflies bear different meanings in different cultures. Who knew? For the Japanese, a symbol of success, victory, happiness, and courage in battle. A harbinger of rich harvests. Italians believed dragonflies were mischief makers. For the Chinese, a symbol of unpredictability, or having no clear direction. Zunis found them to represent whirl-wind like creatures, powerful, carefree, swift, and active. The Native American tradition held a more psychological meaning: "When we've tricked ourselves into believing that the limitations of physical existence prevent us from changing and growing, dragonfly medicine teaches us to pierce our self-created illusions." I suspect at one time or another all of these meanings have lived in me. These flying messengers, such mirrors.

Clearing Space for What Really Matters

My home office was the first and last room to get attention when Richard and I moved into this house years ago. Much easier just to stack the lidded cardboard boxes of client and presentation notes under the wide umbrella of my sprawling oak table. We put the large items in first, arranged and rearranged, so I could go back to work quickly. Bookcases filled with titles approximately related;

the file cabinet, heaved into the closet, the only spot to be hidden from view. I honestly didn't have time to care that the wall behind my computer was papered with knickered men in knockoffs of old advertisements, under a dark border of golf balls and clubs. I didn't play golf. I figured I'd get used to it, like background noise.

I exempted my office from any renovation; I couldn't afford the time for disarray. As life is wont to do, space gets filled. Over just a few years, with the good and bad news of an expanding client load, the bookshelves overfilled, the boxes of files mounted, and the sorting fell off the to-do list. I moved through my days noticing and not noticing what surrounded me. But at least I got a lot done, and the piles were neat.

The weeks between finding a lump and removing it required a clearing of calendar and mindset. In a similar and very different way, the immediate took precedence. The C-word had a way of making other priorities pale. Meetings and trips got cancelled to make room for test after test; most everything surrendered to the narrow availability of necessary specialists. New materials to study and notes from doctors' appointments inched their way onto shelves and tabletops. The time, surreal as it was, flew by, filled with climbing the steepest learning curve of my life. Once I selected my team of surgeon and oncologists, the process of paying attention was a given. Life seemed to hang in the balance.

Throughout the months of chemotherapy, I lacked the energy and will to undertake any major projects. I protected my space and time for the work of healing, allowing few visitors who would need to spend the night. Just too much for me to get my foggy brain around. Multi-tasking capability vanished along with my old work pace. Life got very simple, very quickly. Even so, weeks were full. Richard did double duty on anything requiring physical strength and mental acuity — most everything to keep life going. I wrote. I cooked. I healed in all the ways I knew how and prepared for radiation.

My husband planned a solo cross-country trip to meet our new granddaughter and celebrate firstborn daughter's 40th birthday. It would be his first break from months of caregiving, and I encouraged him to go.

His timing perfect, my brother unexpectedly called and offered to visit. A couple days alone with my brother hadn't happened in decades; I knew it would be fun!

I totally forgot about what it might mean to let my brother loose in a house that secretly begged him to upgrade. We did make time for wonderfully long conversations, laughs and tears, and we concocted amazing healthy meals, embellishing our mother's touch. Truth be told, I had decided to redo my office even before he called. It was time. Blessed with more energy now that chemo ended and a grace period before radiation, I wanted to mark a chapter change. And I envisioned the space from which my new work would emerge. I wanted what was inside me and around me congruent. I saw my office wall as metaphor: covering what needed to be changed — even if with appealing art, only perpetuated a numbness to what was in front of me. It was time now to make the sanctuary real; time now to claim my own creative voice. Words like *open, simple, inviting, calm* led the design.

We measured the wall, and headed to the wallpaper store. He agreed that the pattern Richard and I had recently spotted would work.

All I had to do was wonder aloud with my brother about how difficult it might be to remove the room's border and wallpaper. I don't remember which of us initiated the pulling at the old corners, but it happened. Too hot to be outside anyway, we launched our mission. Walls stripped bare, heavy burgundy valance discarded, we transformed a wall, which began to transform the room. My brother did the heavy lifting; I measured, cut and managed the water trough to release the glue. He massaged the strips into place, perfectly.

He removed the kitchen valance while he was at it, granting me permission to broaden my view and let in more light. We never did walk on the beach, and I know we both worked harder than we expected, but the experience was holy and worth it. I sat alone among the displaced stuff, catching my breath, discerning what would speak in this new space. I wanted the quiet background to double as foreground, keeping vivid the memory of my dragonfly companions the last several months and my ease that attracted their landing.

The day after my brother left, I bought the paint. I moved the light ladder, turned up the volume on soothing music, and began to commune with my walls.

Unexpectedly I was given more time to finish the redo. My oncologist called with results. A recent MRI, required to clear the way for radiation to begin, signaled a yellow light. Another biopsy was in store. With each stroke of the paintbrush I inhaled joy and exhaled worry. It became a roomful of meditation moments. When my husband came through the door later in the afternoon, he found me balanced on the top rung of the ladder, painting the ceiling tray, calm.

~~~

Meeting with dermatologist today to look at a mole on my head per the surgeon's suggestion. Another biopsy!

~~~

Slowly and carefully over the next month, as I waited for new biopsies to heal, I cleaned out my office closet, de-cluttering shelves. A friend had told me about "Desert Day," an annual monastic rite of Benedictine nuns. They designate a day to remove everything from their rooms, and then make decisions about what gets put back, all or part, being prayerful and mindful about the selection.

Inspired to dedicate a day to this, I chose what would grace my walls and invite me to keep my spirit open. The yet-unframed mandala I drew some years ago, but abandoned to the closet. My beach sunrise photograph, matted in a blue that better complemented this room than the kitchen where it hung. The two oils Richard painted for me, *Surrender* and *Transformation*, that came to fuller brilliance when I turned on the lamplight beneath them. And the treasured black and white photo of an elderly woman walking with her cane along a stone passageway, a large nest of kindling balanced on her head. Inscribed on the back of it: "There are many ways to carry a burden." It was a colleague's gift of gratitude for my own heavy lifting of client work. It continues to speak.

In the space above the windows, the wooden sign: "Simple is Good." Dangling below it, moving with the air, a small mobile dancer holds on to the tail of a butterfly-shaped kite, splendid green. And over the opposite door, a two-foot "Giggle" spelled out in brushed aluminum.

The sorting process is not easy. Things are things. But I have carried with me mementos of experiences and people who formed and loved me over the years. I collected phrases that inspire me, pictures that cause me to look and look again. Eclectic, not store-bought, one-of-a-kind markings of an incredible life. So I get to choose what is just enough, and not too much, to inspire my life going forward. To honor the space. To make me feel invited in, rather than demanded of. It's a balancing act, always. In the choosing, there is a bidding farewell. There is a handing over, a retiring of well-worn, not without a cleansing of tears. I am making space for the new, by being lighter of foot and heart.

After sending a short email to my circle of support about the biopsies, a new period of waiting.

A client wrote:

You are forever in my thoughts and prayers. Yesterday I saw a poster that read, 'Applaud Courage!' If you could hear me right now, I am clapping my hands together for you as you again wait for the results of a biopsy. It's got to be a challenge to keep your positive energy going when you have to maneuver the next thing and the next. I am sitting at my home office desk, and my puppies think I am crazy, not understanding why I am clapping. I am also praying, praying, praying.

And another client wrote:

I had hoped you were there, meaning through the tunnel by now and into the sunshine. I am sure you were so hoping, too. I am apprehensive as you must be, but hopeful. I join you in prayer. 'Throughing' the tunnel is probably more true. For all of us.

And another:

I've attached a picture of one of the sunflowers my children and I planted in your honor, shortly after we learned of your diagnosis months ago. We have transplanted them twice. As they grew, the underneath leaves that didn't get much sun withered and fell off; the top leaves grew healthier and stronger as a result. I have thought of you each day as I watered these flowers.

Today I noticed little yellow finches landing on them, eating the seeds out of their centers. What a feast for these little creatures! I couldn't help but think the birds were getting nourishment from the flowers the same way you have nourished us spiritually throughout your entire journey by sharing your days.

And last weekend something truly amazing happened! We were making our annual trek up to Wisconsin, a pilgrimage I've made since the year I was born. This year, however, while driving along the highway, I saw for the very first time fields and fields and fields of sunflowers! I was overwhelmed with joy! I was picturing you when you got recent news that a newfound nodule was benign. I made my husband stop the car on the highway so I could get out to take pictures and send these to you!

Dear ones:

I am still celebrating the end of chemo, and benign results on two recent biopsies, and am looking toward radiation treatment. Thankfully, the hematoma resulting from one biopsy is getting reabsorbed, and the site is healing.

Richard and I met yesterday with a gem of a radiation oncologist. During the appointment, I listened to the technical language the doctor used, and heard the metaphor in it. "Data from the scan is used to define the 'point *of origin'*— the place you start from, and then you guide from there. Then you find coordinates, so the movement of beams can be calibrated, targeted, adjusted to keep essential organs safe." It's very precise and delicate work to aim accurately, moving neither too close nor too far, preserving through a process of destroying.

As I expected to hear, the site around 'the second lumpectomy,' as he called it, needs to fully heal before we start radiation prep procedures. So my next appointment is in three weeks, and if the site is healed, then a CT scan will inform the planning for radiation. I was glad to hear today that healthy cells repair themselves, but cancer cells do not. Thank God.

I am grateful for the amazing resilience of the body and how much mine has worked to rebound from the onslaught of chemo. It is living through the cycle of destruction to new creation. It's miraculous to me. Some side effects persist, but they are minor in the scheme of things.

love, amy

Happy Birthday Balance

Most every one of my mornings since diagnosis begins with thanks, but my birthday this year marks an extra special celebration of being alive. Some people dread singing to a year older: may I never. I'll take becoming over the hill after these months of prolonged steep climb.

I begin with meditation. God turning darkness into light and making the crooked ways straight. Then I bike the winding way to the beach early enough to join the sand in welcoming the sun. What a glorious time to walk that stretch of beach from the inn down past the locked and lonely mansions to where sea oats wait. There's the point closest to the sandbar where I like to see the terns, where surf and creek meet each other coming and going. I accept the oncologist's warning to be careful: tomorrow is my radiation dry-run. A bloody slip on an oyster shell is not in my interest. I content myself to skinny dip my feet in the shallows.

Rumbling around in my head as I walk is how unable I am to gauge the amount that satisfies a day without reaching the tipping point way too soon. I acknowledge changes in energy level and ability to focus. Everything takes more time. I wonder how this state of too-full is even possible, given the hours I used to dedicate to a different kind of work. *Am I reluctant to claim healing as work, requiring its own time?* When I do "real work" I am not inclined to take the time to sleep, eat, exercise, or generally take care with the kind of regular commitment I now know. Thinking I need to accomplish more than heal from another biopsy, and strengthen for a barrage of radiation, becomes its own form of tyranny. Or denial. Such an urge to **do,** lest I run out of time.

I walk on and ask myself: *What would change if I changed the frame — to feel worthy of balance instead of working to achieve it?* Such a fine line between allowing what is, and striving to get it right. I am surprised at the words that came to my lips: *God, I offer you this imbalance right now.* This admission of being as I am, less-than-perfect, brings some peace.

Once back at the inn, I turn up the wooden steps to the landing where my bike waits. Against the rail, I dust the sand from my shoes and look up. Twenty-two high-flying geese initially move in a line, then as if on cue, into formations across the sky. I take the time to watch. One pattern looks like an L, then a capital I, then a V, then something like a question mark. I don't put it all together at first, but as I unchain my bike, the spelling hits me: *I get to add the E! How then shall I live?* Whatever the meaning in the sky, whatever the way ahead, I begin another year to discover how to allow the balance. I start by getting back on my bike and head home.

Dear ones:

I hope wherever you are, you are braving this summer heat. I am grateful for air conditioning that can handle the load here in South Carolina.

I find myself wanting to fully immerse in a life not focused on cancer — feeling myself released in a way, and yet there remains the responsibility to attend to healing. The pace that I can tolerate without getting fatigued is much slower than what was familiar. Even getting used to a new healing rhythm takes some doing. I am no longer living life in cycles, anticipating one good week out of three. Now, each day feels relatively good. So the choice point each day is made more poignant: **What do I do with my life's time? How do I direct my energy? What stays, and what goes?**

I am noticing the courage it takes to deliberate — to not just quickly or unconsciously put everything back as it was, over-full, distracting.

Here I am now. **Am I going to make it through?** is receding. Some uneasiness remains about the acute and long-term effects of this much radiation, but I have to trust. A friend advised: "You worry about your worries. Stop it!" Patience, never my strong suit.

It's just a lot easier to make the transitions mentally than emotionally, at least for me. My yoga instructor said last week, "You are in charge of the intensity of your movement and how long you sustain it; use the breath to support you." I used to live not paying attention to my breathing. Shallow or held breath was part of focusing outward, pushing through stress, mustering strength. Now I am learning to rest, enjoy and give thanks in that pause between one breath ending and the next starting. As I reread the truth of what I have written to you here, I ask myself, **Who IS this person emerging from the cocoon?**

This past weekend Richard and I spent the first day at the beach, and with doctor's permission, I waded into that warm ocean water, spotted a couple dolphins in the distance, rocked on gentle waves. Ah, home. I wept at the sensation, at the utter normalness and specialness of it. I felt a bittersweet joy, knowing that once radiation starts protection against infection will be critical; I won't be back in the ocean this season. A worthy sacrifice.

Thank you for continuing to be in touch with me, for praying for and with me, for sharing in the delight and depth of life. Let's continue together to raise our awareness to all who suffer, sending them love for healing. It has worked wonders for me, but I am just one of many.

love, amy

Eight
Aiming True

When the mind plays tug-of-war, rope burn feels more like frayed nerves and pressing fatigue. It doesn't even have to be big things vying to force the off-balance. One side can be waking up crabby after another night of fitful sleep. The other side can be the hint of upset about a change in routine, even if it's a dear friend's arriving from across the country for a few days' visit. Or sometimes, it's just mental stew.

Everything I do seems like an opportunity to practice staying open to what presents.

After a morning of necessaries and some journal writing, I decided to take a short walk on this cloudy day. Then, an outdoor shower—a gift, living in the south.

As I stood with my back against the massaging water, my eyes closed, I heard my internal debate. The press to do more with my days, to push more to produce and accomplish. And its counter: *Isn't it enough to focus on how I am being faithful through this crisis, documenting my way and sharing that? Isn't this serving?* My mind, the relentless judge, must have been persuaded; the push-pull of anxiety ceased. As I finished the question, I could feel the sun on my head, its first time poking out from the clouds. As I opened my eyes, a circle of rainbow surrounded me, perfect; mist greets light. Droplets of water flipped off my back and shoulders onto the colors, as though opening a fugue, contrapuntal, staccato, bright. The words *showered with grace* came to my mind, and I took this as affirmation. *Yes, even now I am enough, and enough is plenty.* I laughed out loud in pure joy, amazed, delivered. I wrapped my just-right-size periwinkle towel around me and stepped out to the rest of my day.

Learning to Take Care

So weird not to be living in three-week routines now that chemo is over. I feel released! And yet, how to live with this new freedom? Not having to anticipate a week of feeling wretched, the slow comeback, and then a week of more or less full life. Now, day after day is like that third week. A new kind of sameness. My mind fills in, starts to assume continuance of one good day then another. How different my intensity when attending to moments I assume will persist, rather than be taken away. Perhaps humans can sustain that level of noticing for only so long. Or, we need to practice, practice.

Dear ones:

Yesterday Richard and I met with the radiation oncologist and got the green light to make preparations for radiation.

It takes a team. The oncologist consults with a physicist and a dosimetrist to plan how to aim the radiation beams. Both art and science: geometry of size, angles, dosage all blend in an effort to accurately target the right tissue, and avoid touching the very close lungs and heart. I told him to take all the time he needed to work a flawless plan!

You'll appreciate this. At the dry-run measurement and simulation the oncologist will put permanent marks called tattoos on my skin where the beams will aim. "Souvenirs," as a friend named them. When I asked the doctor if I could get dragon images, he laughed; I told him I'd always see the dots as dragons anyway. Why not scare any proliferative cells to bits at the thought of reclaiming my body?

Stay tuned.

love, amy

~~~

My radiation oncologist smiled at the number of questions I brought in with me to my first consult with him since treatment started. A great exchange. He offered, "Isn't it amazing how much we take for granted, how much passes us without notice in the fly of life?" The wording landed.

I shared with him how grateful I am to be able to take the time to notice — both old and new things, in new ways. He gently chided me, "You have learned about not living like a fiend! A fiend thinks that more or faster or next is the best place to be."

He counseled me to plan on a full year after treatment to rebuild, to be fully back into life and on my game. This truth jolted me. So different were my expectations! After many tearful minutes of letting this all sink in, I realized how important the advice was. I would naturally expect a lot of myself and assume a return to full physical strength soon after treatments ended. I get it that disappointment creates its own stress, and an unrealistic timetable can set back full healing. I admitted to him, "I am doing rehab now and am exhausted after lifting a nine-pound bar!" So much for considering I could *heal* like a fiend!

I am learning to live life on my own terms, but not under my usual conditions. I see how my familiar assumptions constrain me. Looks like the weeks of radiation will offer me more practice to stay awake.

Welcoming a New Way of Moving with Power

In another visualization process with my friend guiding by phone, I was invited to imagine a place where I might get initiated into a different way of being powerful in the world. My road warrior days had taken their toll.

I chose as my special place the Bow River in Alberta, Canada, near the conference center I worked the year before. I imagined that I walked through woods to an opening, then onto large rocks to cross to a sand bar in the middle of the shallow river. I stood with snow-capped peaks surrounding me, crisp fresh air filling my lungs. I opened my arms and looked upward, eyes closed, silent. A burst of sunny white light appeared, then covered and warmed me like a soft gauzy robe.

I began to run around the perimeter of the sand, with my right hand swirling, directing, splashing down into the icy current, while my left arm stretched upward, hand open to the sky. The two sides of me were in different motion: one, active, even frantic, sometimes easy, gathering up and giving back, stirring things up in the process. The other reached above, yet ruddered me. I noticed my stance wobbly, my moving arm, tired.

I paused, wondering how to bring more ease, while standing strong. Warmth flowed down my left arm as I lowered it and wrapped it around my right. I saw myself hugging myself, as if cocooned. I changed my stance, rooting firmly on both feet, feeling the power in my legs, in all of me. I heard from within: *This is my beloved daughter in whom I am well pleased.* I cried at these words, the possibility of this peace.

As the time came to turn back to the woods, I felt myself springing effortlessly across the rocks. At the last few feet before the shoreline, I saw myself leap from a rock onto what looked to be a hand, and then off the ends of the fingertips onto the land. I paused again, then walked through the woods, light of step, my body warm.

117

After completing the visualization exercise, I sat in my office in silence, surprised at what images came forth. Truly I was being invited to examine my way of moving in the world, to bring the sides of myself into better balance. I felt myself blessed by Spirit speaking through me. A new power and lightness of being by adjusting my stance, and opening my arms to my own belovedness.

When someone deeply listens
I can hear my heart speak.
In ways and words
I didn't know lived in me,
I can find my way through
questions, fog.
When someone deeply listens
I can feel her eyes looking through mine
calling my soul hesitating to be seen:
"Come."
I can read in her face
permission
to feel beloved.

A week later…

My therapist greeted me wearing a dragonfly necklace! We had never talked about a mutual regard for these creatures. I knew when I saw this sign we would wade into the murky water where dragonflies like to hover.

Indeed.

These last months I drafted my funeral service—a task I had not put on my to-do list until diagnosis, but today my therapist invited me to design a ceremony to mark a spiritual awakening and welcome myself as I emerge into a new space of living. She framed my choice: to focus on what was no longer or learn how to rest in the ambiguity. To accept the disorientation without trying to change it. Such a rich paradox here: less effort provides more ability to find footing in the wilderness, that in-between zone between my former and future self. How well-worn my tendency to want to overdo, push through, act rather than open to what comes. It is not second nature to me to know how surviving this ordeal and living with less effort fit together.

Some days the learning in this journey is offered in mythic proportions. *Can the warrior in me, who knows that kind of strength, actually hold hands with the priestess who acknowledges grace? Can those two parts of me come together and help me move through this space of living in-between? Can drive and flow co-exist, or even thrive together?* No longer who I was, not yet who I will be. I get to redefine now what it means to be achiever.

We talked through what I learned with clients about transformation. Bottom line: it is not easy nor clearly defined. It requires intention, integration: take what is useful from the current way and commit to evolve more fully. That can involve coming face-to-face with what was avoided for years. Or easing up on the reins clutched tightly for success. My old warrior way of doing, or overdoing, or thinking I had to do it all myself, is yielding to a different kind of reliance. Trusting, opening, and relaxing, quite different from effortful.

I know effortful. It has been my default for years.

How does a more balanced me live? Who knew that my diagnosis could comprise a prescription for fuller life, even as I realize the lessening of it in some ways?

Addressing all this with my wise and loving therapist, I could feel a new ease. I realized I can choose to *rely on*, rather than *achieve* this: *To trust the unfolding, to rest in abundance.* "Amy, that is seeing with Divine Eyes," she affirmed. I was moved by her words, grateful.

I took those eyes home, and let the insights settle as I slowly, mindfully, made myself lunch: a brown rice risotto with fresh shitake mushrooms, shallots and parsley. And a salad of fresh greens. I sat down and randomly opened the book my therapist lent me. These words faced me: "She discovered she was the one she'd been waiting for. Celebrate her self-reliance." *Oh my.*

~~~

When I read emails about the pace my family, friends, and clients are living these days, I wonder how this life rhythm meshes with the balance I am learning now. The relentlessness of my prior work pace seems foreign territory. But I also am finding out how I can create relentlessness anywhere, in any role. I find myself even now having to hold myself back from getting immersed in volunteering.

Saying 'no' is still hard. I so want to return to feeling normal, and a constant 'yes' has been my normal. Exerting effort means I am passionate, alive, even if frenzied. Now I am learning to trust myself as a channel for the life living through me. Like breathing in yoga that actually opens my body to move. The more I push and cling to a definition of life and identity not healthy for me, the more I know fear is taking the lead. Who knew what courage it would take to say yes to balance!

~~~

This week grief wells up inside me as I feel deeply the loss of health and work I loved. There are fewer steps and less information to manage in radiation compared to chemo, so this is the ebb after the flow. I am surprised at how just under the surface my tears are now. Here, at this relatively easy chapter of treatment, I am having a harder time emotionally. As though the time is now ripe for another level of realizing the weight of it all. Although I believe the beginning of the rest of my life means closing well on what came before, I admit that living all these levels of ending, while having the physical energy of a stone some days, seems daunting. I sang at church yesterday, "Grant us wisdom, grant us courage ..." with tears running down my cheeks.

Seeking to Live Lighter

At today's local meeting of cancer survivors, an oncologist presented research on Chemo Brain. Insights kept jumping into my head. Yes, my brain is functioning differently right now. It's hard to follow conversations. It takes me a half hour to write a paragraph. There is so much I can't make sense of with my usual reasoning.

My creative side is flourishing, though. This part of my brain is patient with word delays. It generates images I use to understand and frame deep questions. I feel myself living in a thin place, lightly attached to this material plane.

Paradoxically, I am more prepared than ever to let go of this life, even as I fight to keep it. I guess it's not a surprise to feel ambivalent about re-entry. A hearty commitment to re-enter life after treatments makes me wonder: *Will deeper attaching to **this world** bring on the pain of having to let it go all over again in the future?*

It's hard to sustain the right spirit of balance—to be in the world but not of it. It has been so easy for me to attach to this life and live unconsciously—as though "we have all the time in the world." I will not be able to believe that again. I realized today that my strategy for re-entry needs a healthy balance of attachment and detachment. That's the only way I can consciously love this world and leave it.

~~~

My mind is churning tonight. *Is my calm so fragile?* This time is so filled with paradoxes. Living in the present, while being intentional about the future. Surrendering to a bigger plan unfolding, and fighting to live. Making plans, knowing they are likely to change. To be certainly committed to healing, even though I can't be certain of the outcome. Not being a prisoner to expectations, yet does having no expectations signal a lack of confidence about my future? It doesn't take much for fear to loom large: *Can my cells interpret my questions about re-entry, and the possibility of recurrence, as my not wanting to get well? Do I believe strongly enough in my healing?*

Tonight through an avalanche of tears, I told Richard about my churn, my fear. He wisely offered that this mental maelstrom is about control. My over-analyzing (hardly new for me) gets me stuck in the questions. He asked how

I could be lighter, "lightness being the way to surrender to a very big God." Our conversation gave me respite, space to settle my mind and heart.

Before going to bed, I created affirmations to tell myself out loud what is true.

I know I am worthy of living my life cancer-free. Cancer will not define me. I am light. I am making healthy choices in my healing. I do not need disease to feel ease.

In my guided visualization today, I began with the question, *How can I live my life now, in a lighter way?*

I imagined being in a grove of trees in the Oregon fog, just inland from the coast. Off the path through the trees, I spot an area of soft yellow-green moss, sheltered. I sit. As I breathe, I see a shape, changing from squiggly lines of energy to something like a dragonfly, reflecting on its wings some sunlight breaking through the fog. I reach up to touch it, but I am not sure if it is part of me or outside of me.

I ask it how to proceed on the path. *I am not planning to sit on this moss forever!* It says to me: *Just get up and start walking.* I say in return: *Just like that?? Just walk? It's so foggy!* It repeats the instruction.

I get up and start walking, seeing only a foot or so in front of me. *This is how you do it*, the image said. *If you are committed to the walking, you watch out for rocks or loose material on the path. You won't know if a wild animal or butterfly will find you. Pause and take stock of how it's going, but just keep walking. I am part of you. When you forget, I will help you remember how to walk.*

As the visualization ended, I found my face wet with tears. On my knees, I thanked this messenger, and the path, and the moss, and the fog.

Leaving my fifth radiation treatment today, I joined Richard who was sitting in the car, reading, waiting, windows open. When I got in, something large and dark flew in my window, and I ducked instinctively. A few seconds later, it stopped flying and landed on the ledge, perched against the lock button. A pea-green-headed, blue-eyed dragonfly, torso striped chartreuse and black, with burnt sienna tail, black wings. He rested there, like he belonged.

As Richard started the engine, I raised the window a few inches to free him to fly off and to spare him the onslaught of full moving air once we got underway. Expecting him to leave, I watched him stay, even bracing himself as though he wanted to watch the world blur by. He stayed and stayed and stayed.

On the bridge over the Intracoastal Waterway, I raised the window all the way, and still he stayed. Silence and cool air inside the car refreshed us all. I noticed the detail of him—the head tilting sideways, the cross-shaped markings painted down a segmented tail, the exquisite laced wings. He rode next to me those thirty minutes, as though on mission. I watched him as he watched the landscape, gentle and still.

We pulled into our garage, and still he stayed. I asked my husband to fetch my camera. The dragonfly obliged a pose. I rolled down the window, opened the door, and got out, and he held fast, as though waiting for me to leave first. I faced him, nodded, and thanked him for the amazing grace of his presence. He may have thanked me for the ride.

After breakfast, I went back into the car to take a look. He was gone. I felt a mix of momentary relief, a pang of sadness that the visit had ended, and a surge of joy at the mystery of it all. It doesn't matter what of all this was intended. I will not forget this fellow traveler, biding his time, modeling ease in foreign terrain.

~~~

My friend wrote today:

No one can predict the terrain of emergence for another. Pay attention to what sparks and what deadens your energy. Take notes. And wait.

I noted in my journal: Such a wonderful terrifying mystery to live in the moment.

~~~

As I waited today for some photos to print, I was surprised when my dad's voice popped into my mind: *Meet the ball!* His words brought back a childhood memory of his repeated instruction during softball practice. It meant keeping my eye on the ball, seeing it through the moment when bat and ball meet, and not getting distracted to look where the ball might be going. It meant not trying to kill it on contact — my usual mode, but just meet it. The ball goes the distance by hitting the sweet spot on the bat. I haven't recalled this in more decades than I want to admit. But, how apt the advice is now. I closed my eyes there in the photo alcove of the store and playfully assumed the posture again, leaning into home plate.

Gone now over three decades, dad smiled, I believe.

Later in the day, I admitted to the radiation oncologist: "I pressure myself with thinking it's up to me to not have this cancer recur." He smiled and assured me, "Dr. Webb, you are NOT that powerful!" I heard that.

He did reinforce the smart and helpful practices that **are** in my control. Ah, yes, stay the course. Find the sweet spot. Meet the ball.

Learning Together to Transform

How important this prayer group has become for me. I remember vividly its conception. Just after diagnosis, when a fellow parishioner initially suggested I invite a group of people to meet and pray with me regularly through my treatments, I responded with, *People will really DO that? I can ASK for this??* Now I know that without my yes to his invitation, I would have deprived my healing and theirs.

Eight prayer group members have been my confidants. They pray and hope with me. They bear witness to my changing states of mind, body, and spirit, and offer their honest and loving feedback. They implicitly hold me accountable to be present to it all, to not miss the meaning in all this. With them alongside, I see how everything I experience serves to fortify what wants to be open, loving, aware, and awake, while continuing to walk into the unknown.

Today they arrived at 4 p.m. I updated them on what I am learning through the breath and energy work I am doing. We talked about acceptance and how hard that is. How in the face of difficult passage, we each do what we can do, while struggling with the illusion that we can control the outcome.

We talked together about the huge paradigm shift for me these last months and how challenging to reconcile the tensions of transition:

Build structures that provide stability and support while knowing that people, practices and routines change.

Feel fully the rollercoaster of medical and emotional cycles, but try not to dwell in the depths.

Attend to my body's needs and limits, without obsessing.

Acknowledge the fears of whether I will live and commit to live the life I have.

Open to signs and messages pointing the way, and step out blindly amidst all the ambiguity.

Experiment with alternative healing practices alongside the tried and true, without working to guarantee an outcome I think I "should" have.

I can't help but see the contrast with how I lived life before. I relied on control, assuming to some degree that a life of familiar plans, schedules, pace and routines would hold. These months have upended this certainty. Life-altering lessons in letting go.

One of the men stunned me with this comment, "How you've gone through this journey has taught us about transformation. Please write, because we are all being called to transform." I hadn't expected the extent to which my sharing the steps of my walk resonated with the unfolding of their own life stories. No wonder the root of the word sacrifice means to make sacred. Right now my writing is a way of mapping my journey for me. But if walking my way is light-bearing to others, I am open, willing, ready to be a lantern.

Dear ones:

Halfway through radiation now I am doing fine, just chronically tired. I daily choose to surrender to life in low gear.

Each weekday morning I leave at 7:30 to drive a half hour to the cancer treatment center. I drive myself, unless too tired. Something about feeling normal this way. And I use the quiet of the drive to pray, listen to music or poetry, or just take in the view. My usual summer rhythm of walking an hour in the early morning has been interrupted by this treatment schedule, and it throws me some. I am amazed at how much of a routine I had created and counted on through chemo cycles, even in these months of non-routine. I have to push myself a bit to exercise, but daily cardio and regular rehab have rewarded me with

being able to keep my eyes open past 7:30 pm now! Absolutely incredible how easily a day fills, a week fills, even without the more than full-time job that used to occupy center stage of my life.

The radiation session itself is quick. Funny, the things I've adopted to cope. Rituals, of sorts. Like asking if I could use the same gown each day to have something that is a constant through these 30 treatments. And I wear each day the earrings my sister made for me. And I choose magazines in the waiting area with articles that energize rather than scare me.

I'm grateful for the quiet and calm and loveliness of the treatment center. At least in early morning, there are only a couple of us sitting on quilt-draped rocking chairs, waiting to be called. I get on that table without stress (in fact, my blood pressure is lower than ever in my life), and I wait for the short-bursts of buzz. I am helped to a sitting position quicker than I can finish a short litany of prayers. So, I've chosen one prayer while on the table—
AIM TRUE!

I give myself over to trust, that all is happening as it needs to right now, and my part is to show up and not get in the way.

I met with my radiation oncologist this week. All looks good. And I made the choice about what drug support I will have for the next five years or more. None of the possible side effects are pleasant, but so it goes. At least my hair is growing back, salt and pepper, heavy on the salt.

Daily I am experimenting with cooking healthy things, reading, writing, praying, exercising, corresponding, and getting engaged in a few community or church activities that invite what I can do without draining my energy. Time with Richard is precious. We are in sync. We are finding out about aging bodies sooner than we anticipated, but life is still full. I don't feel denied. If anything, choosing wisely and selectively how to use time continues to be the challenge. Even in this Siberia of sorts, there is so much life to live. So many options that can please or consume. We take ourselves with us, whatever the state, don't we?

Enough for today. I continue to feel buoyed by your prayers and presence. Thank you, bless you. Pray for all who are suffering, and live, live, live!

love, amy

Nine
Crossing to
What Lies Beyond

I don't know how to answer your question **Then**
what? *about life plans after radiation. It's a day at a
time. I will give myself time to recover my energy and
rebuild muscle strength. I am making a list of things
that interest me for the next chapter of life. It still
feels so new to even be able to write the next chapter
of life.*

This is what I wrote to a client who has received my
updates throughout, and is already thinking ahead for me.
But even without this prompting, my mind automatically
moves to question what follows treatments. Can't rein that
mind in so easily. Such a life urge to want to keep moving
forward, whatever that is. I understand better now how
being in the moment, and focusing on my healing, is
EXACTLY where I need to be, but there is also a pull to
feel purposeful, to find a spot to put these new lessons to
good use.

Thinking about purpose launches me into thoughts of
DOING rather than BEING. My pattern of living ahead of
myself, trying on new ideas and actions. *Ad nauseum.*

These days, fielding questions by colleagues and friends about my next chapter fuels this old urgency. I read something today by Viktor Frankl: "You don't create your mission in life; you detect it."

I'm still tempted to want to create from the outside in, rather than discern from the inside out. I need to pray more, think less. I hear in myself, *Amy, allow what you need for healing to lead you.*

~~~

I wrote to a friend today:

My kitchen looks like a pharmacy, but I've got the rhythm down and welcome it. I'm committed to a regimen of rehab exercise: a more active cardio workout, critical stretching, walking and yoga. I'm amazed at how weak my muscles are and what they will need to replenish.

Living into the Mystery

I shared with my priest today my uncertainty about where to put my toe back into the water of work life. I know I don't want to go back to the pace I knew, but I also know I am still in the cocoon of treatments and recovery.

During our conversation, an image came to mind of me struggling against a cocoon from the inside, trying to either hurry or assist the new life to emerge. I seemed to be resisting the natural order of things—trying to shove myself out of its hold, rather than being patient to fully form. As if a butterfly needed help to free itself! I laughed.

I was seeing the cocoon as limitation and was missing that it protects what's developing from external distraction and threat.

As we talked further I heard myself voice worry about not being able to re-gear myself for new work or even regain a semblance of the energy and passion I used to have. All these iterations exhaust me. Real as they are in my mind, they serve as distractions from doing the work at hand — to close well on this healing process. I am being asked to be patient, to allow the chrysalis its time.

Tonight as I journaled this exchange, I realize *I have always lived my life in a series of plans. It's a whole new deal to live into the mystery of it.*

~~~

In today's visualization exercise I asked the question: *Who is emerging from this journey?* Again, lying on my home office floor, I was guided to breathe deeply and relax. I imagined sitting in St. Patrick's Cathedral in New York, a place I regularly visited to pray when in that city on business.

I sat alone in the quiet at first, then imagined a close colleague and my dear grandmother sitting in the pew in front of me. I asked them why they were present. They gifted me with the words: *solace, acknowledgement, another way.* My colleague soothed me, turning and touching my face, offering a knowing consolation for the work toll, and a deep understanding of my passion for the work. My grandmother then said, *Look where you have come with your life. This is why you needed all these experiences — to catch up with yourself!* I recalled vividly her sitting in my bedroom when I was in the eighth grade, listening to me read an essay I wrote that I shared with no one else. She had asked then, "How could you write this? You haven't lived long enough to know all this yet!" Now she was helping me connect those early insights with this journey home.

They moved back to join me in my pew: *We will wait with you.* We sat a good while until a man came up and handed me a basket — large, with a tall handle, purplish white, filled to overflowing. I took the basket onto my lap. The contents spilled out all over the floor. As I bent to pick them up, my colleague counseled: *No, these don't all go back in your basket. You get to decide what goes in the basket. And maybe you will use the basket for what can flow through it, rather than to carry things.* I found her comment strange, but I pondered it. After several minutes I saw the basket fill with yellow light, which warmed me all over. It was flowing out through the slits in the basket's weave. I took this in, silently, and a revelation came to mind: *This basket does not have to contain a lot of things. It does not have to confine the contents it holds. It's more of a vessel.* We all admired the basket and its light.

As the time came to leave the church, I hugged my colleague and grandmother in gratitude, put the basket around my left arm and walked out the door. No one else in the church could see the basket, but I knew I was carrying it. When I got outside, I was surprised by a sense of having new eyes. I looked at what I was carrying and realized: *Oh, it's a lantern, not a basket!*

~~~

The next day, I received this from a friend:

When people experience the suffering of another, it is always through the lens of their own experience. People show up in powerful or subtle ways. Sometimes people will react to you in ways that appear clueless or unsympathetic; some may treat you as if you were leprous, as if having cancer is a disease they might catch if they get too close. The reality of your disease can hold up a mirror, and looking into it can bring up in others all kinds of fear.

I may not understand the experience of cancer since I have never had it, but I have known deep loss, and I can empathize with the humanness of your experience. You, too, are deepening your capacity for empathy just by sharing what you are going through. And you find ways to soothe others in the process. Your asking us to pray for people suffering everywhere is profound. I am just grateful for the mirror you are being.

~~~

I learned today that the essay I wrote a couple of years ago, that I finally submitted, was accepted for publication. Sometimes we muster the courage to put our vision out front and let it pull us. Sometimes we hold the light for others to see their way. Sometimes we become aware that a vision beyond our imagining is already at work, and we can only see it when we open and take the first steps.

Have Mercy!

Tonight I went to a meeting to discuss the possibility of obtaining a dragon boat for our local cancer survivors. I planned to get better acquainted with those interested and their mission. Instead, I met a group struggling to organize. After observing and listening a good while, I offered to step in to help frame the issues. That turned into an invitation to lead the meeting and facilitate a discussion of strategy and steps. Four hours later, the group was on track, and I felt satisfied about being potent after a wilderness of wondering if I still had something to offer.

But as I drove home, I realized that in saying yes to that invitation, I had chosen to say no to dinner and scheduled pills, awaiting me at home. How easily I can get carried away, overriding my body's signals. Such a dance to balance it all: accepting my need to be purposeful and my need for care.

~~~

A dear colleague—the same one who appeared in my recent visualization about the basket of light, called this morning. In our conversation I relayed the experience of getting swept up in last night's meeting, ignoring my own needs. I confessed my frustration over not "getting it" about how to calibrate. Two steps forward, one back. Still too inclined to run past the edge of sense, having to correct after-the-fact as opposed to mid-running. She calmly listened, then offered something that took my breath away: "Amy, have MERCY on yourself!"

I sat in silence. She stayed in it with me, unable to see the tears flowing down my cheeks. How unlikely it is for me to show myself mercy, or even consider my need to do so. Another invitation here: find mercy to fully live.

Possibilities
open and shut me down
leaving me parched —
a desert can't hold
too much rain falling too fast.
Where are the oases
clear and fresh and real,
not mirage?

Still, I walk,
sun baring relentless light,
so strong it blinds,
sandstorms of questions
grit my peace.
Is pressure to persist
the same as freedom?
Maybe.

To another friend, I wrote:

Overall, with this period of time and practice, I have gotten much better at saying no. When I am tired, I cancel what I've committed to for the day and rest. New for me to do this: I don't want to let people down, or seem undependable. But now I know I can't give on empty. And I can't live on empty. I am equally worth tending to, and my relationships deserve the truth. It makes me think twice about what I commit to, so I don't have to cancel a lot. It's a shift in thinking and seeing, and how I move through my days.

Emerging

This time of both considering what might be a future beyond treatments and not wanting to live ahead of myself, seems another instance of surrendering to what is underway. My intention for my visualization exercise today: *What is the quality of life I desire after all this?*

Again, after preparatory breath work, my guiding friend asked me, "Where are you now?"

I imagined myself sitting on a dirt floor within a large concrete cylinder, about four feet wide, eight feet high. Hugging my knees to my chest, I noticed the rough-textured walls, their cracks and crevices and uneven places. Beside me was a single ray of light. Feeling content at the moment, but wondering how long this would be enough, I didn't know how to take the next step.

As I described this to my friend, she asked if there were anything I could do to change the picture in any way. I breathed. I imagined standing up inside the enclosure, hesitant. Then I remembered from real Outward Bound experience how I learned to scale a granite wall. I imagined feeling that courage again and found what would serve as toeholds along one wall. I began to slide, brace, leverage, scoot my body. At the top I stood upright and looked out across a great distance. After a pause, I looked down and saw myself sitting with someone on the ground, listening to her stories. As the person finished and went on her way, I discovered that this cylinder served as a container to feel safe within, as well as a means to see beyond, and to connect with another.

What would it be like to leave this? Again, my friend guided: "Stand outside the cylinder and look back at it for a moment, to see what it represents from that angle." Grateful for her nudge, over the top I leapt, landing safely on the ground beside it. I walked forward a few steps, turned to it. I saw it as a short monument at first, but the image morphed. I was astonished to see it take on the form of an inuksuk! *Do I dare hope to see you as this way marker, offering direction for those walking after me who feel lost?* The new form responded: *Take your stand in that place, then walk from it. You don't need an inuksuk if you are not on the journey.* In that moment I felt grateful, calm, yet uncertain about what was ahead. I turned and just started walking. I trusted I would find what else I needed to learn.

I shared this visualization story with my prayer group today and admitted my swirl over the next chapter of "work" after treatments. We discussed how doing the next right thing, if it is caught up in duty or self-righteousness, can get us off center. I can spend a lot of energy trying to figure out what "right" is. But if I consider doing the next *peaceful* thing, that might change my choice of action or manner. This discussion brought to mind a recent fact my radiation oncologist shared: Stress releases hormones that act like in-body steroids, inflaming what they touch. *My whole body needs the next peaceful thing.*

One of the prayer group members asked me at the end of our meeting, "What if you changed your query from 'What is my work?' to 'What are my gifts?'"

~~~

I had this image while driving home from radiation today. I saw myself standing empty-handed before God, receiving the *graciousness of grace.* Those were the words that came to me. I realized God doesn't need anything I have; I will transition from this life with nothing. Being receptive to the grace of each moment is nothing less than impossible, but something I'm given to do.

~~~

I've gotten used to getting timely messages from all sorts of sources. This morning again, a dream became messenger.

I dreamed I was hearing a voice telling me what I needed for healing. I was focusing hard to get the spelling right. The voice spelled out *A-S-T-R-A-L-A-G-U-S*. I could see the letters clearly, but was unsure of their order or meaning. I awoke.

With a still vivid recall after a cup of green tea, I went to the computer and typed in the letters. It corrected, "Do you mean 'astragalus'? Its meaning: a powerful supplement designed to fortify immune function. I was stunned. I had never heard of it nor read about it. I called my nutritionist and shared the dream and asked if she knew about this. Not only did she know it, she had planned to suggest it when we had our next scheduled call!

I know we are part of something much bigger than we can know.

Celebrating the Way Through

It's quiet as a cathedral in the middle of the day and as dark inside. The front doors of the Yawkey Cancer Center slide open in greeting, morning after morning, welcoming me. Twenty-eight times so far. The lobby lights haven't been turned on yet. I am first in line for this communion of tender tissue and penetrating beam.

Barely awake, I head down the hallway, toward Dressing Room A, on the right. I know its placement of chairs and corner table with perky brochures, tissues. The lounge chair waits for my purse (if I remembered to bring it), then shirt and camisole. I've carried the same gown in with me daily, clutched as a prayer shawl. I know its texture, scent, stamina, like a uniform that offers something secure, consistent. I feel fine in this humble garb, blue trim.

There is a community here. Someone, like me, is nearing the end of her treatments, another with nine more to go, another just starting. We meet at the rocking chairs and greet each other with silence or hello. Today I remember years ago walking along the early morning streets in Roncegno, a town in northern Italy. I had passed a resident sweeping the sidewalk with a handmade broom. The words "buon giorno" had brushed the air between us. Quick, perfunctory, shy, as though meeting eyes and stopping to speak would interrupt the rhythm. Not so here. Sometimes there are only moments to share a sentence or two before a name is called. Sometimes in the waiting there is time to read or pray. We each do our readying. Each person is a story of surviving, and we witness that in one another. One man has a 20% chance with his inoperable condition; we pull for him like a brother.

"Mrs. Webb, come on in," the technician invites. Beyond the heavy door marked with the danger sign for radiation, a short hallway leads to the lead-lined room with all the computers, massive machines, overhead sunrise mural. I offer a "buon giorno" of sorts, kick off my shoes, and walk over to the table to position myself. Left arm up, hand in a stirrup, I feel held. Right side still, hand holding a fold of my gown. Left side undressed, exposed, with colored lasers aligning on the X. Today, music in the background: "These are the good ol' days." I laugh at the ridiculous truth of this. With one treatment to go, I know I will miss some of this intimate routine. I feel a kind of melancholy I wouldn't have imagined.

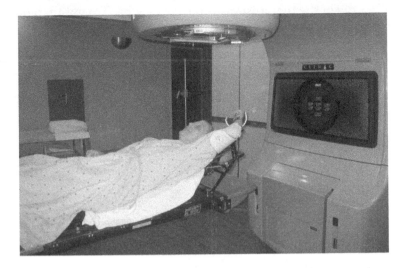

These last five "boost" treatments have a different configuration. For the first twenty-five, the large grey circular machine that shot x-rays through me rotated to my right, stopping just off my cheek, and then moved down to the left, below the plane of the table, carefully, precariously, angled. I saw through closed eyes the image of a sun rising and setting, with my body the horizon line. Now, there is only one machine position for the electron boost. It looks more like a satellite dish, with a long camera lens aiming down on me.

As the therapists leave the room before the radiation actually starts, they always cheerfully promise, "We'll be right back." I take comfort in this practice. I am alone only moments with those dangerous and potentially life-saving rays. Bbbbzzzzzzzzzzz, pause, align, bbbbzzzzzzzzzzz. Seconds later, a deep breath when it's over. I hardly had time to get used to being flat before being helped to my feet. This movement, like the flow of yoga, signifying how all things change, moment to moment.

One of the therapists asks me today what I'm going to do to celebrate the end of treatment: "This is big. You've gone through a lot. You have to give yourself a lot of credit for getting through all this." I hold back tears at both the reality of the ordeal and its end in sight. I start to wonder what would be a worthy celebration. *Maybe a massage once my skin has healed.* Grateful for this encouragement, I'd choose something. "See you tomorrow," she promises, one last time.

Richard drove me to my last radiation treatment. Just before the bridge over the Intracoastal Waterway, at the point where one typically could see clearly ahead, only fog was visible today. No bridge. No sky. Headlights on. All of a sudden lights became visible on cars heading north opposite us, exiting the fog. How perfect the metaphor for life! Clear is just that short distance immediately before me; what lies beyond, foggy. I get the message here: *Put your lights on and go. Enter the fog. Trust the bridge before you. Keep moving.*

Richard waited the few minutes in the car. I went into the treatment center and was greeted by a chorus of "Happy Graduation Day, Mrs. Webb!" After my last buzz, I received a new gel for my skin rash and hugs all around, staff and waiting patients alike. I walked back to the car with the lyrics "I'm free!" popping into my head. Richard opened the door for me and handed me a congratulations card, including a gift certificate for a massage. And we both hugged and cried.

As we re-crossed the bridge heading for home, I called Richard's attention to sunrays breaking through the fog.

Dear ones:

Amazing how the mind adjusts to stages
of peril, eventually. Now at the end of this
period, I admit a bit of anxiety. Treatments
were tough, but I knew what they were for
and accepted their presence and timetable.
After-effects will be what they will be.
Anxiety creeps in, however, when I imagine
the "protection" being different—the irony
in calling such assaults protective!

Months of regular treatments yield
to a daily anti-estrogen pill, my own
attentiveness to a healthy lifestyle, and
whatever. It's the whatever, the unknown,
which gives me jitters. I do take solace in
"God of the present moment, be with us."
But the paradox remains: soon it will be
time to leave "house arrest" and "get my
groove back," as friends say. It will be time
to make plans again while knowing full well
that we are only given a day at a time.

I am better and worse for these last months.
Something I read last week struck a chord:
"For cancer survivors, good as new simply
does not pertain." True, I am getting better
at focusing my energy toward doing the
next peaceful thing, slowing down enough to
be more mindful of moments. I am praying
myself down from the top rung of the worry
ladder after I leap there hearing stories of
recurrence. That worry may someday move
fully to the back of my mind, but not yet.

My spiritual exercise has been making peace with death, while living life full-out. Learning to let go of the illusion that I can power my way through my days and win postponement points with the grim reaper. "All is well, and all manner of thing shall be well"; thank you, Julian of Norwich.

I walked through Brookgreen Gardens with my camera today and watched a caterpillar get to the end of a stalk. I leaned way down to get close to him and saw him lean way out on that stalk, attempting to find his next foothold. Right, left, up, down, he reached and paused again and again, with nothing close to grab. Finally, the front of him dropped, suspending himself in air, while his back legs kept walking. Eventually he dropped lightly and fully onto another stalk. He landed in one piece, probably not where or how he expected, but he kept on walking.

That's what I will do. I am committed to do the walking, while leaning in and letting go.

love, amy

Ten
Trusting the New Return

Tonight Richard and I lined the driveway with paper luminarias to commemorate Breast Cancer Awareness Month—and, timing amazing, the end of my treatments. Such a milestone! In the bottom of each pink bag I put a handful of sand from the beach and a votive candle. He helped me light the candles at dusk, and we sat on the porch steps watching the darkness fill in around rows of light. Certainly, a night vigil in support of a cure and in memory of loved ones lost to this disease. And for us, a celebration of life. *I AM HERE*!

Earlier in the day, I sent an update:

Dear ones:

Today begins the first week of post-treatment, and, the first day of Breast Cancer Awareness Month. It feels like a new beginning. Nearly nine months of labor and now it's time to move gently into the life that this past period has prepared me to live. I am most grateful for a new day, and so I commit to be conscious and present in it. I will continue to heal, reclaim robustness, savor. I want to bring into daily practice the lessons I've learned about living with love and ease. I know for certain I will remember how important my relationship with you has been and is: "It is in the shelter of each other that the people live." (Irish proverb).

I now have a graduation certificate: "Merit and appreciation for the highest degree of courage, determination, and good nature," signed by my radiation oncologist and his wonderful staff. I already miss them, and the fellow patients. But I'm home for the first Monday in six weeks. I look at my eyebrows growing back, and hair Richard trimmed for me this weekend — signs of renewal after a long climb. Everything changes, perceptibly and imperceptibly. I am grateful for our traveling together through the changes that have marked my passage. I know you are with me through the days to come, and I appreciate your continuing prayers. God knows you have been and are powerful manifestations of grace for me.

I learned something today in reading the recent issue of **Spirituality and Health**. The Hebrew word for 'thank you' is **todah**, which also means to admit. Healing involves both.

> When we say 'thank you' we are making an admission. We admit that we needed someone else. To say thank you means to admit that 'I couldn't have done it

without you.' Beneath it all, when we express our gratitude, be it to other humans or the Divine, we are recognizing our dependence on another. And though that dependence is never easy to admit, when graciously acknowledged, it facilitates harmony, bonding, freedom.

So I say to you wholeheartedly: Todah. Grazie. Danke. Merci. Gracias. Thank you! Such a journey — such a threshold, this has been. I will be in touch as time goes on, to celebrate milestones and provide relevant news. Many of you have encouraged me to write; I will honor that call in time. I hope to bear witness to some landmarks through this crossing that help me answer, **What was THAT about!?**

In the months and years ahead, may we be conscious of the time we are given. Enjoy! May we continue to touch wondrously those lives with whom we are privileged to travel.

I love you, amy

Healing Forward

Moving out of treatment phase and on my own for prevention seems like that time after a funeral, when all the absorbing activity is finished, and the survivor is left alone with the reality of loss and fear.

At my first post-treatment follow-up, my radiation oncologist asks, "Are you healing?" I didn't know how to answer. I teared up thinking *I trust that I am. I am doing what I know to enable that.* I confided how it feels like I am living in a new body, a stark contrast to a year ago, before diagnosis. A constant adjusting of expectations and pace. Each day a discerning, a calibrating of too much and just right amounts of doing. I criticize myself: *REALLY? THIS little bit of activity is too much!??*

He listened long and well, and counseled:

When others ask, 'Are you back?' you can bravely answer, 'Not yet.' It's hardest after the structure of treatment is over, when you finally realize the extent of what you've been through. There's no gauge for knowing how far along the healing is. Measures reveal only so much; outer skin heals faster than the inside. Listen to your body to tell you where your limits are, and back off a tick. These edges aren't fixed; they will continue to shift. Give yourself a break; it's only been a month. You're free of cancer. Now, it's about learning.

Grateful, grateful, grateful for his wisdom. For his *seeing* me. I see more clearly that it's mine to determine what is in my best interest, day to day. It's not a linear path. Yesterday, a mile walk; today, a half. What was normal may no longer fit. I remember a client who confessed he had to quit running marathons because he couldn't learn to run slow enough. I get to choose how to run the marathon that is my life: quit or learn. I'll learn.

Chemo and radiation complete, I swallowed my first anti-estrogen pill today. This will be my daily regimen for years to offset recurrence. To mark this new chapter, I walked into my office, picked up the stuffed animals that people sent to be my guarding companions, hugged them all tightly, thanked them, and placed each in the basket of other treasures I've collected since childhood. It felt symbolic to invite them to take their place in life ongoing— to be integrated, as I am working to do with the lessons that I have collected this year.

My intention during yoga class today: *I live and love with ease.* Our instructor led exercises to move us through time periods of future, present, and past. We grounded ourselves in a standing pose and were asked to name our strong legs. I named mine *compassion.* As we stepped forward, we shouted aloud one word we wanted to let go of as we faced the future. Then, we pulled back to standing with hands over our hearts, calling out a word that we wanted to keep. I paired *fear* and *faith.* We did the same with the present, moving out to the side with one word, and then returning with another. I chose to let go of *busy* and return with *open.* As we stepped back into past, I called out *resistance* and returned with *acceptance.* Our last pose, the corpse pose, was one of the most powerful ever for me. I clearly felt in my body a spray of gold light filling and warming my arms and chest. I gave thanks for the comfort of this unexpected gift.

Back home as I sat and told Richard about the yoga class experience, the doorbell rang. He got up to answer the door, then walked into the kitchen carrying a huge spray of helium balloons, sent by a dear friend to mark the end of my treatments. They were star-shaped, gold, and they took my breath away.

Over the next days, I watched the balloons hold together as one bouquet, dance with a movement of air, and gently, continually, adjust position.

I actually loved high school physics, learning about the laws of movement and energy and change. I vaguely recall that an object in motion tends to stay in motion unless acted upon by outside forces. And how momentum can change depending on the object's frame of reference, and the strength of opposing forces. Little did I know back then how the concepts would have relevance five decades later to figuring out how to deal with this change of life.

Through my treatments I barely gave thought to what had comprised a more-than-full work life before diagnosis. I focused my energy on getting to the point of being able to ask the questions: *How, then, shall I live? What is to be my work?* I visualized myself moving through various challenges as the countdown to life-after-treatment transpired. Time now to visualize the steps in the transition from this chapter ending to a new one about to begin.

Returning to my former way of working and living felt contrary to what I needed to be able to sustain. Once again, my friend provided the guiding questions to imagine a way to communicate this news to my dear colleagues.

I imagined sitting with them in a circle, facing the reality of the change that changed me. I saw myself talking with them, describing a treasured scene from the opera, *Parsifal*. The protagonist walked out of the forest where he had wandered for so many years and stands, taking off his helmet, placing it on the ground in front of him, stepping back. Symbolically, he was shedding what he no longer needed, readying for his return home. I imagined admitting to my colleagues that I would now be putting down the armor of road warrior to focus on health, husband, community, home. I didn't have a clear picture of life outside the forest, but I had a sense of how I wanted to be in it.

Their resistance to my decision came through: the legitimate protests, judgments, fears. And how I might stand in that energy. After my initial clutch of fear, I could see something deeper operating. I put my hands on their shoulders and acknowledged their grief over losing a connection that mattered. I felt that deep sadness with them, real-time.

Sobs shook me. I had to pause the visualization process a long while to release them. My friend on the phone patiently held the space for me to recover.

My attention returned to the imagined meeting and I saw it shift to a celebration of our decades together. We reviewed travels and experiences and clients we loved, did high-fives with tears in our eyes. And I thanked them for that work—the opportunity, the livelihood, the uniquely dear relationship.

As the visualization session ended, I could feel a swirl of peace, relief, power, and hope, even as I found my body spent. When the time comes for the actual conversation with colleagues, I can trust I will be able to ask for what I need. How we end affects how we can begin. Like Parsifal, I am emerging from this wasteland, to serve with a new frame of reference, new momentum.

~~~

I wrote to a colleague today about what has fortified me over months of treatments:

The simplest things—a call, a prayer, an email, a note. What can anyone say or do during a process like this other than indicate, I am here, we are here, walking together in hope. Each of us ultimately walks a solitary path, but I believe each life can carve messages on the inuksuk for those who follow.

Each person who has communicated with me in one form or another has been a source of healing balm. What an expression of community, connection, shared faith! When we are face-to-face with our finiteness and find commonality in each other's stories of this place, we discover as a collective

*what we most want to hold onto, in all its fragility.
Such a paradox—once we rediscover and reclaim
our fragility, we are more able to see its part in
something larger: our essence, neither fragile nor
time-bound. So many voices, stories, touches
helped me see.*

A couple of weeks later, mid-month, a healing visit...

I am ready, rested; the house is spotless for receiving the little one. The doorbell rings. My heart leaps. I walk to the front door and look out the side window to see my daughter's huge smile. "Open up," she urges. *Little does she know how opened I am!* I pull the door wide. "OOOOOhhhhlivia," I cry. Tears. Lots. I gently lift her from her mother's arms and hold her precious life. She nestles in, calmly, naturally. For this, we have all waited and watched and prayed.

This is what a miracle holding a miracle feels like. She won't remember these days of my welcoming her, cradling her, loving her, but I will. I trust that. When she left wrapped in the quilt Richard's sister and I made for her, I could see how precious she was in all that belovedness.

Releasing

Richard and I drive to the Shenandoah Valley. A long-planned trip to see the fall color in a place we know and love. We take the long drive slowly, with plenty of stops for me to stretch my body. We agree we want the time to be together hiking the national park, drinking the tonic of rolling hills and fresh air. We have no daily agenda, no push; instead, we listen to what our bodies need, some walking, reading, a warm bath, deep conversations. He observes that

I am more subdued, less intense, less obviously attached to certainty, and tells me: "We are moving toward death as kindly as possible." Paradoxically, death has a new presence for us. Not as ominous now that treatments are finished, but reminding us to attend to how we want to live.

Different as we are, we are good together. I met the word last week, "convivienza," meaning to take up with one another. It comes from root words meaning feast and live. Not simple to put a life of new days together while coming back to life, but natural as sun and storm.

Last night we did something totally spontaneous and new. We went to the Haunted House at the local fire station. At several points on the walk through the dark tunnels, I fell backwards into Richard's arms, screaming out the fright, legs shaking and wobbling beneath me. As we exited I bent down and put my head between my legs to catch my breath. A couple fire fighters, clearly pleased that their creative effort had such impact, were nonetheless concerned and came over to make sure I was ok. I was. On the short drive home under a black sky of stars, I felt stunned by my reaction. *Was this a kind of capstone?* Clearly this felt like catharsis, finale, liberation—months of pent-up screams released in one night. Throughout the year, my smaller yells that were voiced in the privacy of my office or on walks in the woods, readied me for this discharge. And, once again I knew Richard's strength behind me, supporting me, threshold after threshold, to the exit.

Nearly a year after first hearing about the dragon boat, I get the oncologist's release to paddle. I take my place in line on the dock to secure a life vest my size. Perfect evening, just a bit of chill on the air, heron flying overhead, V's of geese. Seated, hip against the gunwale, facing the river, I plow the paddle straight into the water, pull back, lift up. Form matters. The coach calls the strokes; my throat clutches with joy. "Reach it out" means exert fully, and we do. "Let it ride" gives us a chance to pull in the paddles and rest. Pace matters. I thoroughly enjoy the delicious peach sky reflected in that wakeless water. Like gliding on silver glass. This exceeded what I had hoped for when I was on the other side of getting through.

~~~

Another hoped-for opportunity comes to fruition…

I am not sure what possessed me to do this but months before finishing radiation treatments, I agreed I would help lead a program at church entitled "Strong Women, Strong Voices." The commitment required seven women to each research the life of a strong woman in church history and present the story to an audience. For weeks before the program, I wondered if I had been unrealistic in my plan to participate. My hair had barely grown back, my brain still struggled to retrieve words and put them in the right order, my voice stuttered. Nonetheless, I chose to stay the course. I wrote out the words, and trusted. And I practiced and practiced.

Today, standing at the podium, I spoke my first paragraph, wobbly legs and all, quoting from the book written by the woman I selected. As I began to hear my own strong voice, my courage seemed to mirror hers. Little did I know when I signed on for this how it would serve as a turning point in my confidence.

Another Kind of Ride

Chemotherapy and radiation behind me, I committed to my rehab to get my strength back. Three months into this new routine, on a warm December afternoon, my phone rang and a voice called out: "Suit up; it's nearly 80 degrees! Time to ride!" During my fifth chemo appointment, a fellow breast cancer survivor had promised me a ride on her Harley. At that time, the idea of it seemed forever away. I couldn't fathom it then; I was trying to survive and she was talking full-out thriving. Today my trend of cautious restraint gave way to spontaneous. Time to let out the throttle a bit. I put on some jeans and a sweater, hiking boots, and the biker's cap from a client. Off I went.

I hadn't been on the back of a good-sized motorcycle since my early 20s — that flying-upside-down chapter of my life leaving me a bit scared of those machines. Too young and too full of myself the first (and last) time I tried to drive one, it drove me. Up over a curb. Too heavy for me, it fell on its side, taking me and my future daring with it. But I missed ducking butterflies on deserted back roads.

I pulled into my friend's driveway, where she readied the beast. I donned her too-large leather jacket and just-right helmet. Before we left, she took a picture of me from the back, both arms raised, fingers forming peace signs. Then I held on for my dear life.

We ruled the two-lane highway for about twenty miles. Holding firmly but loosely around her middle, I felt the tug of fear. As I gained trust in the driver, my body remembered how to move as one with her, and I relaxed my grip. By the time we stopped on a side road to check in with each other, I knew I could not turn back yet. I borrowed her cell phone to call Richard. He laughed out loud, asking if I'd be home before dark!

The most Carolina-blue of skies radiated gorgeously, with generous puffs of ultra white clouds filling my visor. Everything felt close, fully accessible to my senses: the deadness of the opossum, the pineness of the timbers in the logging truck we followed, the wafting of sweet olive perfume. We passed through country I never knew existed. Acres of dirt poor and acres of forest rich. Houses with front porches filled with all but people, and houses too small for a porch. Past the signs for Hell Hole Swamp, and the one for a lunch special, "Liver and Gizzard Snack, $1.99."

How many moments bless me like this? How often do I notice the bird in the tree close-up? As we rode the last few miles toward home I realized with utter clarity how my cancer experience turned my life into a life of appreciating moments, a kind of tuning fork, inviting my resonance. It called me to attention, inviting me to live with an attitude of *carpe diem* while making smart choices about energy expenditure and nourishment.

I get to choose bottled water over a soda and when just enough stiffness earned today might make tomorrow more manageable. I get to decide what and how much to say yes to and when. I welcome my new lease on life.

All of it.

Today's last-minute jaunt. The decades-old ordeal of motorcycling in the pelting rain; the revolting task of picking bugs out of my teeth after the long ride. Even the one a few short months ago of hearing the oncology nurse intone, 'Deep breath!' as her needle the size of a drapery-hook found home in my port. It all says *notice*, and *say yes to the ride.*

Dear ones:

I'm learning about what this recovery period entails. How perfect for me that it parallels the Advent season. Waiting, watching, preparing, persevering — the promise of light after darkness. So much is provided about the treatment time of this disease. For nine months, I have sensed what to expect, what to do, what could be. Now the work, the worry is different. Routine now is To-Be-Determined. This recovery time, another in-between.

Last night, a musical performance at church. Well into the program, as a girls' ensemble took their place on the riser, I

---

watched a troupe of mourning doves land
on bleacher-like branches of the live oak
outside our sanctuary window. They stayed.
Motionless. Paying attention. At the end of
the sweet "Silent Night," they flew off, but
I believe we all took those words of calm to
heart. From "Behold I Tell You a Mystery" (in
Handel's Messiah), My cells heard the truth of
these words: **And ye shall be changed.**

I wouldn't give this year back. I have had
the time and inclination to see and hear
and feel the everyday miraculous. To
know suffering on a new level, and the
compassion and patience it has yielded. To
be closer to the Divine and conscious of the
continuance of grace.

I know I have been changed. I also know
it's not about what I know; it's about what
I trust. And I know I trust the mystery to
continue.

Peace to us all.

love, amy

Eleven
And the Walk Continues

Through the months of enduring through treatments and recovery, my photo-taking not only documented for my journals and supporters my stages of change, but also gave me a sense of wonder through it all. I slowed my walk. I explored the richness within the limits of my home and yard and a two-mile radius for more months than I ever imagined. There was a rhythm and life in the looking that buoyed me. As I became drawn to subjects opening, I opened. The right focus, the right distance mattered, as did knowing when to stand utterly still. Some days I took the pictures sensing my photography-loving mother looked through my eyes. When I lost my way, thinking the road through hell might never end, my photo journal's remaining blank pages reminded me that there was more noticing to do. My writing, my camera, would get me moving again. Those healing arts kept me paying attention to what lived beyond the anxiety in my head.

My passion for creating in word and picture didn't end when my album pages filled. It didn't end with treatments or through recovery. Seeing deeply, opening to what arrives, became a new and ever-changing lens for my life.

Meeting Friends Again in Bronze and Stone

Richard and I visited Brookgreen Gardens today, specifically to visit this year's sculpture award winners. I remember how powerful the experience last year, just days after diagnosis, discovering that the sculptures then on exhibit embodied the states I was living. It seemed at the time such an improbable but essential coincidence.

Now, six months after my treatments, we walked through the gallery doors to find awaiting us: "Dawn." "Blossom." "Breakthrough." "Discovery." "Tale of Respect." "The Blessing."

I wept with joy. I wanted to hug them. I wanted to sit at the foot of their pedestals and share stories. I thank God for new eyes: *OF COURSE these are the ones that are here!*

~~~

A week later, over tea with my priest, I raised the questions inside me about my re-entry from this forced retreat: *What will I return to, and how? How to live into this life tension, balancing my desire for passionate engagement along with a contemplative mind?* She suggested, "In that tension is the possibility for grace." Amazing how just a few months ago the fears I had voiced to her were more about making it through what may be a death sentence. Now, I dare to fear about what the other side of this sentence holds. What an anxious mess I can be!

She gave me space to voice that mess: *Do I trust myself not to relapse into the old ways? Will I fail to reap the benefits of this sacred time? Will I be able to take this newfound centeredness out into a more active life? Will I get carried away by expectations — mine and others — of what work is mine to do?*

I shared with her my reaction to a recent email from a client, urging me to "push forward." His words did not resonate. I heard myself say aloud to her what I have learned about push versus surrender: *It may not make a difference in my living longer, but in how I truly live. Not forcing, but allowing. Aiming true. Acting and receiving.*

From the conversation, I took something away for keeps. It is both invitation and discipline to live moment to moment, listening and responding, rather than defaulting to an unconscious reaction to go do. This is such a critical reframe for my life: this way of taking care of myself IS being closer to God, and that is hardly selfish.

~~~

A few days later, the timing perfect for my occasional therapy appointment, we pick up the theme of balance. This afternoon's session, as usual, powerful, on point. My yoga therapist encouraged, "Give yourself to the paradox: IT ALL IS. Meet any negative or critical thought with, 'Oh, you're here again. Come on in and have a cup of tea.' Start with kindness, gentleness, compassion. Then affirm the positive, the counterpoint."

I felt the heat rise and release in my body, while her hands guided my back muscles to relax. From inside myself I heard the words *core...center...trust...heart.* It felt so right to end the session in the full prostration pose, bowing and releasing all that I am, and am not, to God.

Designing and Trusting

In a phone conversation with a former client today, he commented, "You've had a front row seat to transition, haven't you?"

As we talked about his transition to retirement, I found myself typing notes of key points, as was my practice years ago during our work together:

Amy: *Some people are afraid of retirement, imagining it to be a state of inner nothingness, the opposite of what consumed or identified their lives. These last months have taught me about chapter change. That space is hardly empty, or doesn't have to be. Living mindfully takes a different rhythm. It's amazing how many opportunities will raise their hands to get attention. I've found that the transition is about choice and pacing and staying open to what comes.*

Client: *"Some people won't allow life to invite them. I've always relied on a plan."*

Amy: *You can't predict the steps. It seems a misplace of energy and focus to learn one particular dance, expecting it to be all you will ever need, or to fret about how well you will be able to dance at a future time. Maybe our focus now through these life transitions is to simply identify the music we love. Dance steps will naturally follow.*

166

Later in the evening, another former client called. His wife had gone to the doctor yesterday—a possible brain tumor. Tests started today. He said to me, "I know I can tell you. You, more than anyone I know, can understand what this period is like right now." It brought tears to my eyes remembering this fearful place, and hearing his reality right now. "I wait with you in darkness," I said. *Amazing how what gets served up can ready us to serve.*

Taking on, Letting Go

A few months after radiation, a client I haven't been in touch with in a decade called to invite me to work with him on a leadership development project. He had no clue of my past year of "work."

I felt productive helping him think through strategy and design options. My brain was tracking better on some days, my stuttering less pronounced if I relaxed. I declared that I would not travel after an initial meeting with clients, but would be willing to provide coaching via telephone. Exciting as it was to imagine getting back into professional work again, I knew it would be a challenge to balance the time for this along with my healing regimen. All in right proportion.

I chose to accept the opportunity, defining my terms of engagement, knowing that this project allowed me to work from home. An initial experiment to see how to bring a little of my former work into my new life.

Three months later, hair still growing back and face still gaunt, I met face-to-face with this client group. My first flight in almost two years, deliberately selected because it was direct, short. The meeting went well, my word delays and stuttering not horrible, but inside I felt like a stranger in a strange land. My business clothes no longer really fit me; the weight I lost was more than pounds. My perspective now, lighter. In standing before them, describing my approach to coaching, I understood that I could hardly convey what I know now is essential to move from point A to point B. How much we must shift, forgive, embrace.

What did feel familiar after the meeting, though, was sitting in the plane on the tarmac. Hours. An indefinite delay, mechanical problems—how I remember this space of routine wait when I traveled for client work. Apparently, I needed this experience again tonight, to examine my choices.

I took a deep breath, opened my portfolio and started to write: *What does it mean to become an artist of one's own life?*

I had journaled a while ago about living life post-treatment as a patchwork quilt, but never put the design specifically together. Finding the right pieces would require discerning what to select and apply. What color combinations? Which shapes, in what quantity, and in what arrangement? What textures matter, to make it last longer? Even a crazy quilt has a kind of coherence.

I list wants, not shoulds. Starting with priorities of time with Richard, cooking, writing, photography. I take my time. The list is long, not surprisingly. I'm still me. Sitting back in my seat, reading slowly what I had written, I feel a process come forth from inside me, as if releasing a life form waiting for air.

Like being viewed in 3D, new words emerge from underneath the others: *creativity, connection, stillness, learning,* more. I jot these down, giving them their own column. I sit beholding them, giving them space to breathe. With an urge to play, I write *I am* in front of each quality, turning some from nouns to adjectives: *I AM... creative, connected, still, learning, healthy, beautiful, contributing.* My new list becomes a mirror of how I want to become!

I had intended tonight to use some unasked-for time to be productive, to select the squares of activity and purpose for a quilt of future days and weeks. I hoped the design would help me answer credibly the question: *What did I come through all this to DO?* Little did I imagine that what would be revealed was how seamless the design, how necessary the fit, between who I am being while I do what I do.

It took the plane ride home to finish this. At the bottom of the pages I wrote: *Although I understand that what makes up a living quilt will shift over time, I see tonight that my underlying urge to create will sustain. I want this quilt of a new life to wrap around me, as I adjust it, season after season.*

~~~

Spending a weekend in Charleston with Richard, I attended a Sunday service in the cathedral. The sermon focused on the mythic structure of stories about the hero's journey. The rector, whom I knew, described the stages of transition, from adventuring out, through the wilderness, and then the returning home. I had studied Joseph Campbell's work, trained leaders for years using this structure, and found myself living its truths throughout my treatment process. Nonetheless, I took notes. Until this statement stopped my pen: "You have to simply let go."

At a reception after the service, notes in hand, I went up to the rector. "I have a bone to pick with you," I teased. "I so appreciated your message today. Profound. But... *SIMPLY* let go?? *SIMPLY*??"

He stood looking at me, silent for a minute, then he got it, "OK, maybe if I had said *struggling* to let go that would have been more honest?" I nodded. We laughed. One thing I've learned this past year is how NOT SIMPLE the act of letting go is. And how essential that simple guidance.

Dear ones:

A last big update for a while. I am doing fine, YAY! This month has been a big turning point, with energy and stamina returning.

Yesterday finished the last of a series of medical check-ups and follow-ups, postponed a year through treatments. It was wonderful to hear after my colonoscopy, "See you in 10 years!" My mediport was surgically removed a month ago, a simple operation made easier by singing Happy Birthday to my surgeon while I was on the operating table! Emotional for me to see that apparatus outside of my person. It did its job well; time to bid it adieu. I chose its removal because I wanted to hug Richard without impediment, and I wanted to signal an end to this chapter.

A year to the date of discovering my lump, I had my follow-up mammogram and ultrasound screen. I had so hoped it would be green-light simple. Lying in the dark room after the ultrasound procedure, I thought I was waiting for the surgeon to come in to take out my stitches from port removal. When the mammographer returned for a second go with the ultrasound, my brain knew that yellow light was more the case. I kept focusing on my breathing, meeting myself with compassion and gentleness. Hard as hell, frankly. But I'm better at waiting than I ever used to be. Put that on a resume.

The scan revealed a cyst. The surgeon came in, took a biopsy, and then removed my stitches. Richard, patient through the hours-longer-than-expected wait, heard me whisper as I finally saw him, "No all clear yet."

This was the anxious rhythm survivors speak of, the price of being among the living. It was my turn to wait with grace. Whatever would be, I was determined to put my energy into loving the moments rather than worrying about the ones I may not have. That's easier some days than others.

Four days after the ultrasound, I got the joyous news of "benign." It felt like a piano lifted from my shoulders. Richard and I celebrated with a kale smoothie!

So, now into the dawn of my life. I am committed to my yoga and other healthy practices that have become necessities. Sleep and exercise get on the calendar first. I continue with my nutritionist and will meet with my oncologists quarterly. Ongoing I live with a diet I love, actually. Low amounts of sugar, fat, alcohol; whole grains — nothing processed or refined; when possible, organic, no preservatives, meat without growth hormones. Heavy on salmon, veggies, some fruit. I continue experimenting with foods and recipes. Grocery stores and local farms carry what I need for the most part. I'll expand the garden this summer. Fortunate indeed!

An announcement. After much discerning, I've decided not to resume a travel-based work life. The combination of not wanting the travel stress, regular plane germs, the risk of lymphedema and still-recovering cognitive strength, I want the best conditions to rebuild a compromised immune system. The arrow points to chapter change.

It's been a long wonderful run with the best clients and colleagues in the universe so I admit to this not being anywhere near an easy choice. But I also believe the new will come into view — a different way to contribute, perhaps. I must say that I am still shocked to discover how little time is left in a week if I put first things first, without pushing to cheat time. I still have to adjust my thinking, stop comparing how much I once did with what now feels just-right. And I am learning to drop the guilt when I say no to a wealth of new worthy opportunities.

"You, too, are worthy," a friend told me last week, as I was wondering where to say yes and no. Her statement got my attention. It's a complicated dance to determine how and whom to serve, and where to put myself in the equation. Neither being self-denying nor too full of myself. Now, words like "enough" and "plenty" seem to fit better. I realize there is no end to wants — mine and others. No end to calls to serve.

I am convinced after this ordeal it's not what I do but the self I bring to my days that matters most. Cancer survivor Mark Nepo, whose wisdom has been a companion for me, writes: "There is something about being made less, and continuing, that inexplicably makes the journey holy." So I am promising myself ongoing attentiveness to this holy ground. The first yellow daffodil bloomed in our yard today. As was true a year ago, I was here to see it!

> *Again and again, and never enough, I thank you for being with and for me in so many life-saving ways this past year of recovery. I will let you know any news as I go along. Until then, love and pray without ceasing.*
>
> *love, amy*

Months later...

I talked with a friend about how challenging it is for me to make the time to write. So many things to enjoy now. So much more time is required to maintain health. The patchwork quilt of life I created at the beginning of this year seems to have grown beyond king size! The design I envisioned then didn't quite measure itself against energy or amount of time to live each square with care.

When I admit this her, she listens intently, then asks: "Do you need to do all these things NOW?" Tears well as her question tugs on one I didn't realize I carried: *But how much time do I have?* Ah, that voice of fear. If I allow this voice too much volume in my days, I cannot help but DO. Or overdo. I commit to my friend—and myself — that it's time to tweak the quilt design, drawing stronger borders between what takes up and what gives me life. I get to relax into the time that is mine.

Dear ones:

I awoke very early this morning. Wrapping my hands around a mug of green tea, I looked out my window to see stars, stars, stars. Rather than hurry and change into warm outdoor clothes, I chose to immerse from inside my kitchen, standing against the cold pane, pulling my prayer shawl tighter around me. I am practicing not rushing into more of a moment. The butterfly moves on while one turns and fidgets with the camera.

As I look back on this year so quickly coming to an end, I say again how grateful I am to be alive. Some days it's hard to remember what a year ago was like; some days, very easy. This year of post-treatment recovery had its own ups and downs, forwards and backs. Who knew it would take the time it takes to recover most of me? My energy waxes and wanes, still. Words struggle to come forth; short-term memory takes unannounced time-outs. Focus drifts. Multi-tasking creates a lot of redo.

Health overall is good. Chemo after-effects have me headed with questions to a cardiologist in the New Year. Blood work and bone density are good. It's hard to know what physical changes to report to my oncologist, and what to just observe and chalk up to age. Life feels more muted in ways; I greet it with less oomph and less edge. It's that in-between space that continues to feel foreign: not what I was, not who I will be. Moments unfold; resistance exacts a price.

There is a big part of life-before that I miss, especially since the new is still under construction. I don't miss airplanes, but this new tempo takes some getting used to. It's my typical wanting more that takes me off balance, again and again. A friend asked, "What if life **now** IS optimal?" This reframe has been so important for me. I get a chance to choose how to spend the time of my days. Round after round of that learning.

On Christmas Day, 75 degrees! I walked at low tide to the end point of our beach, where creek converges with waves. Sun spilled in a broad crescent of rays through the mottled clouds. In the distance, a sand bar. All of a sudden what I thought was an edge of sand rose up. Hundreds of birds curved and swirled in an aerial spiral before landing, one after another. Each bird quickly found an empty spot to fill on the sand. As they settled, the view seemed to look the same as when I first noticed, but no longer visible was the change that made up this new picture. The birds had moved, and I was able to behold their amazing dance before they repositioned. I imagined that they were enjoying some sense of community, some nourishment and rest, before the urge to lift and fly again. **Do birds do Sabbath moments? How often do we?**

In my meditation yesterday, these words came to me, **As I am, I am, here.** May we really see one another this coming year as part of the same dance, even as we each do the steps differently. Let us commit to doing what we love, being our best selves, and forgiving ourselves and others when this is not the case.

Bring on a new year! Thanks for your continuing prayers, friendship, and support.

love, amy

Noticing New Connections

All things know their own time.

Just after my year of recovery from treatments, a dear friend and I attended a conference entitled "Sacred Circles," at the Washington National Cathedral. Little did I know when we registered how this content would resonate with my way through cancer, let alone invite an even deeper integration.

When 1300 women from all over the world took a deep breath together and exhaled with an audible sigh, it filled a cathedral with a sound deeper than words.

Women from many faith traditions offered their prayers and wisdom. A Jewish rabbi, bald, with prayer shawl draped over her shoulders, climbed the steps to the sanctuary and opened with a Sabbath ritual prayer. She sang strongly, angelically, the Hebrew words calling us to expand our boundaries of place to where we can really meet one another. A British scholar spoke about her work with the United Nation's Charter for Compassion. A Muslim woman from Afghanistan attested to courageous love in action. She thrived against the odds by claiming "with God's help I find a way." The opening evening closed with a talented chorus of Latina singers, inviting us to sing a refrain about Elegua, keeper of the crossroads, guardian of the path.

Next morning I walked the labyrinth on the cathedral floor — remembering with gratitude other such walking meditations. At Grace Cathedral in San Francisco the day my mother, across the country, was diagnosed with cancer. At Chartres Cathedral with Richard. Inside Point Reyes National Park. At churches and retreat centers. Each experience, different. Each person's unique intention, prayed silently.

Sometimes we get quiet enough to receive. Sometimes the gleanings are profound. Sometimes it's just a relaxing walk. This morning, the sun's angle invites the stained glass to dance on stone pillars, and at my feet.

I take off my shoes. There is something grounding, humbling, to begin by removing what is in the way. I walk to the beginning, voicing silently my question: *How to offer 'yes' to my emerging life?*

As I walk the circuits I first notice how I turn the corners. At one of the turns, an image of a birth canal comes to mind. I affirm: *Yes, my rebirth has required a careful turning of the corners.* When I arrive at the center, I bow deeply toward the distant altar, first with eyes closed, then open. I see the volunteers straightening the seat rows beyond, and a man leaning into his long-handled broom across the painted paths on the grey marble floor. Again I affirm: *Yes, it is all here. As it is.*

I leave the center to wind my way back to where I began. People pause, pass one another, nod in blessing. The reflected colors that had surrounded me, no longer visible. *So soon gone,* I think. My eyes well with tears at hearing the larger truth in these words. Then I hear from inside me: *No, the light is always there. It just depends on where you look when you are on the path. Don't expect to find it in the same place, in the same way.* Tears again; this time, of gratitude.

I am at the last turn before realizing it. Back at the beginning, I stand in place, breathe. *I will remember that with each walk unto my last breath, I will get what I need.*

After the morning plenary session, several dozen of us descend the stairs to the intimate Bethlehem Chapel to participate in a workshop. I try to remember why I registered for this particular one entitled "Feeding Your

Demons." Nonetheless, I am here. The woman seated in front of the altar introduces herself as a Lama, a Tibetan Buddhist teacher. She radiates gentleness, peace.

She invites us to chant a heart-calming mantra that invokes ease and release. We hold our hands out, one open palm representing receptiveness to wisdom, the other an offering of skillfulness. Both of mine buzz from the chanting, and I promise myself to repeat this ritual as I sit to write when I get back home.

She begins by describing the body as a sacred vessel of wisdom, an integration of mind and heart, an "awakened mandala" to listen to and respect:

Mandala refers to a circle containing a complex symmetry, a microcosm of the wholeness in nature, in the universe, in ourselves. The unconscious and the conscious weave a uniquely beautiful design in us, and in tapping into this form, we can meet our potential in a new way.

As I take notes, my mind flashes back to my photos of flower centers that pulled me into and out of myself over the period of my cancer treatments and beyond. I also recalled my mandala drawing class of a decade ago, how my initial sketch unfolded into something new through my moment-to-moment immersion into color and depth and shape. As though it were *drawing me* for hours. I can still hear the instructor exclaim at seeing the result, "A birth!"

The Lama proceeds to tell the story of a man who grew physically weaker as his disease fed on his fears, but reversed course when he changed what he fed them. "Fear manifests as inner chaos, as demons rising in strength when negative emotions or thoughts grant them power. Left unattended, these can obscure the positive indwelling spirit in us." I nod. I know how working with guided imagery partnered so powerfully with my treatments and healing. How it enlivened my positive spirit.

She leads us in a visualization exercise.

I acknowledge that I continue to live with periodic surges of upset that take me off center. My intention now is to understand this dynamic better. She guides us to name our demon. Mine is Agitated Angst. Following the teacher's guidance, I personify the demon growing large before me until I can see its face and feel its force rev my breathing. As directed, I ask it questions: *What do you hunger for? Why are you here?* Through the imagined dialogue I hear it reveal, "*Ease, spaciousness, no cramping expectation.*" As I imagine nourishing it with that ease and spaciousness, the demon calms, smiles, shrinks, until it is replaced by an image of a newborn, secure in a white blanket. I see myself stroking two very soft cheeks. Eventually this shape dissolves into light, into me.

The instructor calls us to open our eyes. Mine are foggy

181

at first. When I can focus, I see the altar in front of me. On it the gold monstrance exposes a white round host. Perhaps my imagined newborn is the Christ child, situated at the heart of the cross! A deep, deep peace fills me.

At the end of the workshop, I walk up to the teacher to confide something I had yet to verbalize to anyone. I tell her about the guided imagery work throughout my illness, and how as this work progressed, I would encounter physical manifestations of the images or colors or messages, sometimes a few days later, sometimes immediately. As though I were living in a thin place between two worlds. These synchronicities had always amazed me, made me wonder. The teacher listens deeply, meets my admission with a nod. She assures me, "Of course! You learned *there is no there out there*. It is all here for us if we open our eyes."

"I know that now," I nod in return. "Every cell in my body is healing with this truth." She smiles, and encourages me, "Continue opening to the divine grace that is real and working through your life." *Making of my life a mandala.*

I leave the chapel and walk to the cathedral bookstore to buy the CD of this guided process to use with my clinic patients. As I stand in line, I notice there on the shelf to my right a collection of primitive crucifixes hand-carved in Africa. I am stunned. On one piece, the face of Christ matches closely the transformed image in my visualization, down to the number of crown points and shape of the eyes. At the heart is the same oval as my newborn, with rays of light emanating from both sides to the edges of the cross. When I remember to breathe, I smile, *Of course*, I say to myself. At one glance, death and rebirth, darkness and light, extraordinary and ordinary. My story, too.

I purchase the piece. I start walking in search of a quiet corner to sit, eat my apple and write.

Epilogue
Finding New Bearings

Eight years later...

I realized a dream to explore the heart of the artic to see firsthand the places where the most ancient inuksuit remain. Hiking on Digges Island in the Hudson Strait, Richard and I trudged to one stand of stones, midway up a hill. An Inuit stone carver traveling with us pointed to another inuksuk up on a nearby ridge. One structure led to another, deliberately positioned to guide a traveler down the hill and across the strait, when a deep covering of snow and ice would make this landscape impossible to read. He translated the meaning of what greets the traveler in these stones:

Where you are heading you cannot see from here, but you can trust this sentinel to be true. Just go in the direction it is pointing, and you will find more there to direct you. No need to worry. No need to wonder where you are, or what is next. Be confident in this: what you need is there, awaiting you.

I stood on that hill, travel journal in hand, wind whipping my tears of recognition, and took notes. My initial resonance with the inuksuk symbol decades ago, which informed my vision during the guided imagery work, had come full circle. It was time to return home and finish giving form to the messages that had carried me and might bear meaning for others.

The Stones Speak

Arctic notes in hand, I sat with a dear friend at her kitchen table, my unedited manuscript in front of me. She asked, "If this story were a way marker, what would the stones convey? What guided your steps?" The messages were still speaking vividly in my life. I readily named them: "Notice. Surrender. Walk with Courage. Connect. Give Thanks." There was no implied order. When an Inuit traveler discovers an inuksuk, the whole of it speaks, even though the individual shapes and direction of stones matter to the meaning.

I downsized my manuscript. I included what would serve as examples of each distinct stone; but, in the process of editing, I saw that oftentimes the themes fit more than one. My experience taught me that each of the stones *are* related, and their messages relevant to not just my story, but to the stories revealed by my circle of support.

Testimony of the Stones

I offer here a summary of the meaning of the stones that marked the way for me. Then, and now. Perhaps they will speak to you.

Notice

When something outside our control stops us in our tracks—a health crisis, a major change, a death, we might shut down and shut out. We want to slam the door, pull the covers over our head, close our eyes and ears, confine the heart. In defensive mode, our bodies want to contract, not expand and open.

If you live, like I once did, as though you have all the time in the world, you might take for granted most every moment you are living. You might also wish away a difficult moment, thinking the present is permanent, forgetting that it is not. All things change. If we can shift our attention to notice what is before us moment to moment, if we can tune into the worlds we try to tune out, we just might see everyday miracles unfold.

Surrender

Experiences we wouldn't have wanted for ourselves, or our loved ones, nonetheless fill some of the time of our lives. More than a tap on the shoulder, each of these can feel like a whack across the head, a kick in the gut. Our tendency, our wiring, is to fight through the threat in order to survive. In much of the literature I read after my diagnosis of cancer, there was a heavy theme of fighting, of mustering all energy against an enemy. Unfortunately, fighting can keep us pressing on with strategies that don't fit the new challenge. These experiences generally call for more than willing ourselves through.

185

The challenge of facing, addressing, and doing the hard work of healing certainly takes plenty of warrior spirit. And there is another side to this spirit that is equally strong: surrendering to what is, rather than living for life to be different. The warrior pose in yoga invites us to stand with arms outstretched, heart exposed to the threat in front of us. Surrender does not have to mean giving up or giving in, but rather fully accepting the situation, knowing it will take more than we can do alone to get through, and freeing up energy to take the next step. Surrendering can open the space to develop new eyes and pay heed to the resources within and around to nourish and sustain us.

Surrender is a courageous act of letting go. Trying to control life is the illusion that seduces us all, in different ways, for different reasons, consciously or unconsciously. That balance of letting go and staying vigilant is one of the toughest to strike, no matter what the circumstances. Surrender requires being willing to learn the terrible truth and beauty of this, again and again.

Walk with Courage

Courage invites us to keep walking when we most want to turn back. Courage is not the absence of fear, but manifests in choosing whether or how to stand in the face of real fear. The hero pose in yoga is difficult; it requires sitting up straight on legs bent beneath you. It stretches and strengthens flexibility in knees, ankles, thighs, and arches of the feet. It reduces tightness and improves posture. Courage is like that: taking on the stretch, risking the pain, to be able to move forward.

I remember my beloved Italian cousin in her late 70s, managing through her own cancer as I was dealing with mine, encouraging me on the phone: "Couragio! Be brave. Don't lose heart." When navigating new and difficult terrain, of course you worry about what is coming around the corner. You wonder if your legs will carry you or collapse in the dark. You feel betrayed by life, self-pitying even, hardly calm. But to live as victim denies the lessons the walk will teach.

There are many ways to find the courage inside waiting to be called into action. There is no one right answer, but I believe we have better and worse ways to make the tough calls. Sometimes we can assume a posture of staring the fear down. Or we can see it as a messenger and ask what it wants and needs. Sometimes we can resist its bullying by daring to find a moment of peace or engage in creative play. Often, we can be surprised at the reservoir of courage inside us, filled up over years of getting to the other side of life-changing pain.

Connect

It can seem only natural in a place of wilderness to feel isolated. Although ultimately we make our way alone, we can find ourselves at an emotional crossroads. We can choose a way that stays open to support and resources along the way, or we can pull in, protecting the self that doesn't want to believe the wilderness will change us. How then do we get through the deepest dark? Some of us are more private than others. We may have learned a hardy self-reliance, or have never been challenged enough to call on a supply beyond our own reserves. Some of us have never learned how to receive, or how to ask. Some mistake unwillingness to show vulnerability for a badge of courage.

The kinds of connections we make in the midst of chaos can be life-giving. Wandering in the dark invites us to connect with our deepest beliefs about life and faith, the ingredients of our resilience, the natural world of which we are a part, and others who offer some light or lift. Paths cross. Even if our survival may be at stake, or the journey not one we ever expected to undertake, if we see our walk as pilgrimage, then it is possible for us to see others as fellow pilgrims.

When we barely have the energy to open our eyelids to the day, we can choose to engage in some way, by paying attention to our dreams, our silence, the birds outside our window, an unexpected visitor, the prayer that is the moment. We can travel in a way that notices the outpouring of grace as real and ready.

Give Thanks

What a difference it makes to take a moment to find something—to find even ONE THING—for which to be grateful. In the midst of grief, or depression, or anxiety about next steps, or in a seemingly endless state of overwhelm, it may take some looking. It may take looking through some new lenses. It might just take suspending your disbelief that there is light in dark.

Credible research now shows how gratitude relates to healing. Our minds cannot hold fear and gratitude simultaneously. The practice of being present to each moment, and seeing what is good or healthy or kind or steady energizes our capacity for hope. It frees us to take the next step by reminding us what is already equipping us. Gratitude begets gratitude.

Some days it's hard to face the barrage of pain, demands, disappointments or unexpected turns in the road. Some days it's far too easy to take for granted the kindness of a spouse or a caring nurse, the wake-up stare of the cat. If we are not attentive to the messengers of good will around us, we may likely assume our own wills are enough. To get through some of the heaviest of storms, with our visibility limited, we find way-markers in a word, a bouquet, a laugh. These can shine us through to the other side if we open to the grace and healing power of gratitude. To pause and practice an art of giving thanks is an invitation to grace.

Dear readers:

I offer you in Stones at the Crossing *my witness to what aiming true looked like for me when faced with a cancer diagnosis. I was forced to stop. I had to rediscover my bearings. The learning, discovering, uncovering, and enduring that I did made its way into something I share now with you, for your own walk in foreign territory. Whatever that may be for you.*

The meaning of the five stones evolved over time. I did what I knew to do, and responded to what wanted to come to life through me. In this book I have described my wilderness trek, labyrinthine as it was. In making the turns again and again, moving toward my center and away, I returned to the place I started. But in the process of walking, I was changed.

189

As I look back over the past ten years, these messages embedded in this inuksuk are what I live by still:

> *You are not prepared, and utterly prepared.*
> *You bring yourself with you.*
> *Vulnerability reveals its own source of strength.*
> *Finding abundance in the midst of limits is*
>   *life-giving.*
> *Moments matter.*
> *A profound partnership is called for—with God,*
>   *others, self.*
> *There are signs along the way.*
> *Practices support.*
> *Expectations get in the way.*
> *Grace is available.*
> *Transformation is possible.*
> *You can do this.*

May my stories inform your way, and lighten your load. But most importantly, may they inspire you to pay deep attention to your own way through. Your turns, and threshold crossings, will teach you, if you are open. You may find different stones as you sit at the base of your own experience, and you may want to share these with others who will walk after you. In this way, may we live and love and learn as fellow travelers, as believers that "all shall be well," no matter where the journey takes us.

love, amy

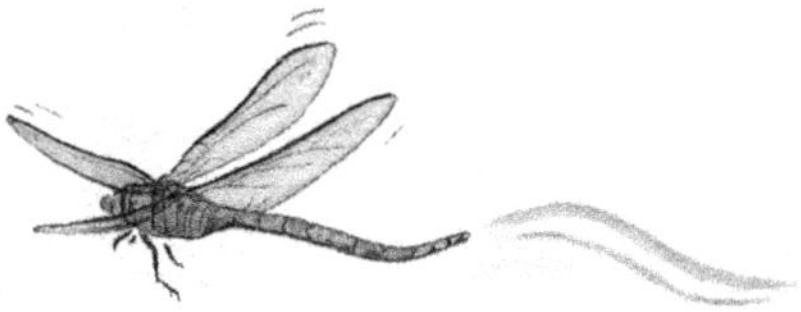

Acknowledgments

Then...

Starting in my teens I handcrafted journals with scrap paper and ribbon—part diary, part collection of musings and memorabilia. I chronicled the decades since. My journaling intensified during my mother's very short bout with cancer, and it steadied me. That writing helped me attend to and honor each minute of the preciousness and terribleness of her passing. Those pages hold what mattered.

So, too, through my own diagnosis and beyond, my journaling served to give witness to my days and help me find the meaning. Unlike old ones boxed in my closet, the journals I kept throughout my health crisis came alive, in a sense. Periodic email updates to family, friends, colleagues, and clients grew to a more regular exchange as the weeks progressed. The insights, encouragement, stories, and counsel I received in return made their way as entries, alongside mine, into my journals. They kept my hope and focus real.

During the final leg of treatments, people encouraged me: "Write the book! Write the book!" I was stunned at the breadth of urging, at how writing itself had become a source of healing. *All in its own time.* But I am glad I kept my journals, notes, emails, and middle-of-the-night ventings, and poems I wrote to my husband.

So I give thanks. Deep and everlasting thanks, to all in my circle of support who took the time to read, pray, laugh, notice, surrender, walk courageously, connect, and give thanks with me. I cannot list you by name here, but you know what mattered so I can continue to live with you in my heart. I thank my husband for his incredible steadfast love, intuitive strength, patience, and clear-eyed wisdom. I thank my team of medical and nutritional providers and staffs. I thank Mary Kay Baker, my bosom buddy; the Reverend Callie Walpole, my priest; Martha Tilyard, my visualization coach; Lisa Rosof, my yoga therapist. I am grateful for the positive energy of the Dragon Boat at the Beach team. And I thank the congregation at Holy Cross Faith Memorial Episcopal Church for welcoming me in weakness and praying me through.

Now...

Finding my way in the murkiness of writing a first book was not unlike aspects of the journey through my illness. True a decade ago, and as I began to write, I had no idea how or where to start. Angst at times plagued me: about doing it right, about what of my experience was worthy or relevant to give voice to, about where to start. There were periods of being just plain stuck, unsure about the next step, discovering how words fail. I worked through finding the just-right distance to see clearly. And, I learned again and again how to get out of my own way.

But there were angels who kept me moving forward, even as I took long pauses to re-energize, or integrate the writing with ongoing life. I thank Pixie Kubeck for her loving persistence in nudging my words out into the world. I thank the readers of drafts for their encouraging and useful feedback, and my dear friend Linda LeBlanc for guiding with honesty and wisdom the reframe of

194

my manuscript. I am ever grateful for my development editor, Janet Hunter, for her expertise, patience, counsel and compassion in getting my work into publishable form while preserving my voice. I thank Bob O'Brien, Publisher, Prose Press, for his generous creative spirit, on-target suggestions, and tenacity with painstaking detail.

Finally, I am grateful for my professional experience with the Center for Creative Leadership, the Canadian Center for Management Development, and Kaplan Devries, Inc. I appreciate the workshops I attended over the past decade at Goddard College, Duke University, The Institute for The Study of Health and Illness, and The Institute for Poetic Medicine. Once again I learned that I was not alone in discovering the healing power of shared stories.

And always...

We begin again. Thanks be to God!

About the Author

In her career as an Organizational Psychologist, Amy D. Webb, PhD, coached and trained thousands of leaders to deepen their capacity to understand and transform their life stories.

Her extensive client list includes Fortune 100 and 500 companies, in industries such as telecommunications, consumer products, and financial services; public sector organizations, including the National Institutes of Health; the Federal Public Service across Canada; and major international companies abroad.

Building awareness and skill, clients learned to lead their work systems more effectively and build healthy connections with others. From decades of this intensive individual, group and team development work, she adapted lessons to guide her through the experience of breast cancer.

Now a 10-year survivor, she continues to discover the extraordinary in the ordinary, and to write about becoming more awake along the way. Her poems and essays have been published in *Sacred Journey, The Journal of Fellowship and Prayer*; The Hektoen International *Journal of Medical Humanities*; *Carolina Grace: Gold for the Soul*; and *Natural Awakenings*.

She and her husband reside in Pawleys Island, South Carolina. *Stones at the Crossing* is her first book.

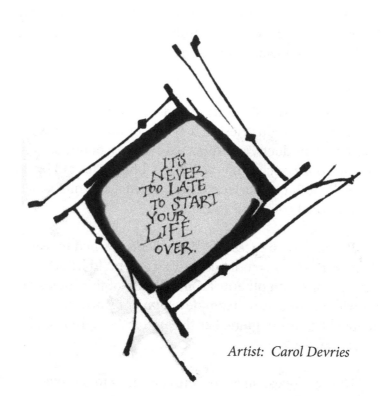

Artist: Carol Devries

CPSIA information can be obtained
at www.ICGtesting.com
Printed in the USA
FSHW022242160120
66025FS